MAGIC
JOHNSON

MAGIC JOHNSON

❧

Sean Dolan

CHELSEA HOUSE PUBLISHERS
Philadelphia

Chelsea House Publishers
Executive Managing Editor Karyn Gullen Browne
Copy Chief Philip Koslow
Picture Editor Adrian G. Allen
Art Director Nora Wertz
Manufacturing Director Gerald Levine
Systems Manager Lindsey Ottman
Production Coordinator Marie Claire Cebrián-Ume

Black Americans of Achievement
Senior Editor Richard Rennert

Staff for MAGIC JOHNSON
Editorial Assistant Nicole Greenblatt
Designer Diana Blume
Picture Researcher Pat Burns
Cover Illustrator Daniel O'Leary

The Chelsea House World Wide Web address is
http://www.chelseahouse.com

5 7 9 8 6 4

Library of Congress Cataloging-in-Publication Data
Dolan, Sean
    Magic Johnson, basketball great/Sean Dolan
    p. cm.—(Black Americans of achievement)
    Includes bibliographical references and index.
ISBN 0-7910-1975-6
        0-7910-1976-4 (pbk.)
  1. Johnson, Earvin, 1959–. 2. Basketball players—United
States—Biography. I. Title. II. Series.
GV884.J63D65 1993   92-21378
796.323'092—dc20
[B]   CIP

For Anne and Brian, the magic
in my life

Frontispiece: *An elated Earvin
("Magic") Johnson raises the
American flag in triumph during
the gold medal ceremony for men's
basketball at the 1992 Olympic
Games.*

CONTENTS

BLACK AMERICANS OF ACHIEVEMENT

HENRY AARON
baseball great

KAREEM ABDUL-JABBAR
basketball great

MUHAMMAD ALI
heavyweight champion

RICHARD ALLEN
religious leader and social activist

MAYA ANGELOU
author

LOUIS ARMSTRONG
musician

ARTHUR ASHE
tennis great

JOSEPHINE BAKER
entertainer

JAMES BALDWIN
author

TYRA BANKS
model

BENJAMIN BANNEKER
scientist and mathematician

COUNT BASIE
bandleader and composer

ANGELA BASSETT
actress

ROMARE BEARDEN
artist

HALLE BERRY
actress

MARY MCLEOD BETHUNE
educator

GEORGE WASHINGTON
CARVER
botanist

JOHNNIE COCHRAN
lawyer

SEAN "PUFFY" COMBS
music producer

BILL COSBY
entertainer

MILES DAVIS
musician

FREDERICK DOUGLASS
abolitionist editor

CHARLES DREW
physician

W. E. B. DU BOIS
scholar and activist

PAUL LAURENCE DUNBAR
poet

DUKE ELLINGTON
bandleader and composer

RALPH ELLISON
author

JULIUS ERVING
basketball great

LOUIS FARRAKHAN
political activist

ELLA FITZGERALD
singer

ARETHA FRANKLIN
entertainer

MORGAN FREEMAN
actor

MARCUS GARVEY
black nationalist leader

JOSH GIBSON
baseball great

WHOOPI GOLDBERG
entertainer

CUBA GOODING JR.
actor

ALEX HALEY
author

PRINCE HALL
social reformer

JIMI HENDRIX
musician

MATTHEW HENSON
explorer

GREGORY HINES
performer

BILLIE HOLIDAY
singer

LENA HORNE
entertainer

WHITNEY HOUSTON
singer and actress

LANGSTON HUGHES
poet

JANET JACKSON
musician

JESSE JACKSON
civil-rights leader and politician

MICHAEL JACKSON
entertainer

SAMUEL L. JACKSON
actor

T. D. JAKES
religious leader

JACK JOHNSON
heavyweight champion

MAGIC JOHNSON
basketball great

SCOTT JOPLIN
composer

BARBARA JORDAN
politician

MICHAEL JORDAN
basketball great

CORETTA SCOTT KING
civil-rights leader

MARTIN LUTHER KING, JR.
civil-rights leader

LEWIS LATIMER
scientist

SPIKE LEE
filmmaker

CARL LEWIS
champion athlete

JOE LOUIS
heavyweight champion

RONALD MCNAIR
astronaut

MALCOLM X
militant black leader

BOB MARLEY
musician

THURGOOD MARSHALL
Supreme Court justice

TERRY MCMILLAN
author

TONI MORRISON
author

ELIJAH MUHAMMAD
religious leader

EDDIE MURPHY
entertainer

JESSE OWENS
champion athlete

SATCHEL PAIGE
baseball great

CHARLIE PARKER
musician

ROSA PARKS
civil-rights leader

COLIN POWELL
military leader

PAUL ROBESON
singer and actor

JACKIE ROBINSON
baseball great

CHRIS ROCK
comedian and actor

DIANA ROSS
entertainer

WILL SMITH
actor

WESLEY SNIPES
actor

CLARENCE THOMAS
Supreme Court justice

SOJOURNER TRUTH
antislavery activist

HARRIET TUBMAN
antislavery activist

NAT TURNER
slave revolt leader

TINA TURNER
entertainer

ALICE WALKER
author

MADAM C. J. WALKER
entrepreneur

BOOKER T. WASHINGTON
educator

DENZEL WASHINGTON
actor

J. C. WATTS
politician

VANESSA WILLIAMS
singer and actress

OPRAH WINFREY
entertainer

TIGER WOODS
golf star

RICHARD WRIGHT
author

ON
ACHIEVEMENT
———— ◖◕◗ ————

Coretta Scott King

BEFORE YOU BEGIN this book, I hope you will ask yourself what the word *excellence* means to you. I think that it's a question we should all ask, and keep asking as we grow older and change. Because the truest answer to it should never change. When you think of excellence, perhaps you think of success at work; or of becoming wealthy; or meeting the right person, getting married, and having a good family life.

Those important goals are worth striving for, but there is a better way to look at excellence. As Martin Luther King, Jr., said in one of his last sermons, "I want you to be first in love. I want you to be first in moral excellence. I want you to be first in generosity. If you want to be important, wonderful. If you want to be great, wonderful. But recognize that he who is greatest among you shall be your servant."

My husband, Martin Luther King, Jr., knew that the true meaning of achievement is service. When I met him, in 1952, he was already ordained as a Baptist preacher and was working toward a doctoral degree at Boston University. I was studying at the New England Conservatory and dreamed of accomplishments in music. We married a year later, and after I graduated the following year we moved to Montgomery, Alabama. We didn't know it then, but our notions of achievement were about to undergo a dramatic change.

You may have read or heard about what happened next. What began with the boycott of a local bus line grew into a national movement, and by the time he was assassinated in 1968 my husband had fashioned a black movement powerful enough to shatter forever the practice of racial segregation. What you may not have read about is where he got his method for resisting injustice without compromising his religious beliefs.

He adopted the strategy of nonviolence from a man of a different race, who lived in a different country, and even practiced a different religion. The man was Mahatma Gandhi, the great leader of India, who devoted his life to serving humanity in the spirit of love and nonviolence. It was in these principles that Martin discovered his method for social reform. More than anything else, those two principles were the key to his achievements.

This book is about black Americans who served society through the excellence of their achievements. It forms a part of the rich history of black men and women in America—a history of stunning accomplishments in every field of human endeavor, from literature and art to science, industry, education, diplomacy, athletics, jurisprudence, even polar exploration.

Not all of the people in this history had the same ideals, but I think you will find something that all of them had in common. Like Martin Luther King, Jr., they all decided to become "drum majors" and serve humanity. In that principle—whether it was expressed in books, inventions, or song—they found something outside themselves to use as a goal and a guide. Something that showed them a way to serve others, instead of only living for themselves.

Reading the stories of these courageous men and women not only helps us discover the principles that we will use to guide our own lives but also teaches us about our black heritage and about America itself. It is crucial for us to know the heroes and heroines of our history and to realize that the price we paid in our struggle for equality in America was dear. But we must also understand that we have gotten as far as we have partly because America's democratic system and ideals made it possible.

We are still struggling with racism and prejudice. But the great men and women in this series are a tribute to the spirit of our democratic ideals and the system in which they have flourished. And that makes their stories special and worth knowing. 🕭

1

"WINNING TIME"

TIME HAD STOPPED. The game's lifetime, as recorded by the amber lights on the not-very-modern scoreboard—no video-screen replays, blaring music, or computerized portraits of the players—was now measured in seconds, not minutes. And there were just eight of them left.

The scoreboard's amber lights also showed the home team ahead by a single point. And yet the sell-out crowd in Boston Garden, the most hallowed arena in the history of professional basketball, was as close to silence as a gathering of 16,000 people can come. They had convened on this May afternoon in 1987, with much hope and a somewhat lesser degree of confidence, for the fourth game of the National Basketball Association (NBA) championship series between their beloved Boston Celtics and the team's perennial rivals, the Los Angeles Lakers.

It was in many ways a privileged assemblage. Above them, masking the bare rafters of the drafty old building, fluttered pennons signifying division titles and the retired jerseys of Celtic greats of the past, as well as the 16 NBA championship banners that the home team had won. Eleven of the banners had been raised during the incomparable golden age of the legendary Bill Russell, two more in the era of Dave Cowens and John Havlicek, and three of them honored the current crop of players spearheaded by

Magic Johnson drives the Los Angeles Lakers past Dale Ellis and the Seattle SuperSonics on April 19, during the 1987 National Basketball Association (NBA) Western Division finals. "My whole game is court sense," Johnson said. "Being smart, taking charge, setting up a play, or, if I have to, scoring."

Johnson's favorite target on the fast break, Los Angeles Lakers forward James Worthy (left) seeks to get around Boston Celtics star Larry Bird during the 1987 NBA finals. The series marked the third and last time in Magic's career that the two talent-packed teams clashed for the league title.

Larry Bird. (The next most successful franchise, the Lakers, had won only eight NBA championships; aside from the Lakers and Celtics, no other team had won more than three.)

Below the crowd was the most readily identifiable basketball court in the world, where the home team customarily carried itself with justified arrogance. The hardwood floor boasted a unique parquet design and a raffish leprechaun logo at center court; the two baskets had friendly and forgiving rims that were beloved by shooters of all allegiances. Some of the parquet floorboards were treacherous, however; they contained dead spots that slowed the ball's bounce and helped the Celtics' quick-handed bandits steal the dribble from unwary visitors.

Performing on this court was a collection of basketball talent without equal in any era. Either the Celtics or the Lakers had played for the NBA championship each year since 1980; the only one of those years when Boston or Los Angeles had not won the title was 1983, when a superb Philadelphia 76ers team interrupted the shared dynasty. The two powerhouses had faced off against each other for the crown in 1984, 1985, and now again in 1987.

These exceedingly spirited contests helped transform the NBA from a league in danger of dying to a universally acknowledged showcase of athletic excellence.

Hoops fans delighted in the playoff matchups between Boston and Los Angeles as the supreme manifestation of the speed, gracefulness, beauty, brawn, and thought that made professional basketball so appealing. Every one of the 10 starting players for the two teams in the 1987 championship finals had been or would be all-stars in the course of their NBA careers. Seven of the players—Earvin ("Magic") Johnson, Kareem Abdul-Jabbar, and James Worthy of the Lakers and Larry Bird, Dennis Johnson, Kevin McHale, and Robert Parish of the Celtics—will in all likelihood be enshrined in the Basketball Hall of Fame.

The least experienced of the 10 starters was A. C. Green, the Lakers' lithe, strong-bodied power forward. He was the team's leading rebounder and its best defender on the front line.

James Worthy was the Lakers small forward, even though at 6 feet 9 inches he was at least an inch taller than Green. Worthy had a huge first step and scored most of his points out of the low post, either on quick spin moves to the basket or a soft turnaround jump shot. He was also the Laker most likely to finish off his team's celebrated fast break (often after a gorgeous assist from Magic Johnson), usually in the form of a dunk, although his were never the pyrotechnic slams favored by other high-jumping forwards. Worthy dunked quietly, with a minimum expenditure of energy.

By 1987, the 7-foot-2-inch Kareem Abdul-Jabbar, the Lakers' center, was only adding to his legend each time he set foot on a basketball court. Just before the start of the championship series, he had turned 40, an incomprehensible age at which to withstand the rigors of an NBA season. And still he excelled; no other player had played so well for so long. By the time he finally retired two seasons later, he had played more games and seasons, collected more rebounds, blocked more shots, won more Most Valuable Player Awards, and scored more points than anyone else in NBA history. Most of those points had been scored by means of the most easily identifiable shot in basketball history, Abdul-Jabbar's famed skyhook, which he launched from high above his head with his body aligned parallel to the basket.

—Byron Scott, the Lakers' shooting guard, was a superb leaper with a flawless jump shot, which made him the perfect backcourt mate for the wizardly Magic. While Johnson was doing what he did best—penetrating and breaking down an opponent's defense—Scott was busy running to an open spot on the floor from which he could launch his jump shot after receiving a pass from Magic.

The Lakers also employed a secret weapon on the bench: Michael Cooper, the NBA's premier sixth man. Whippet-thin and bulldog-tough, he was the league's best defensive player. His specialty was guarding the Celtics' Larry Bird; Cooper was perhaps the only player in the league who could justifiably claim the ability to hold the superstar in check. When Bird conducted the long, solitary practice sessions that had helped make him a legend, he always pretended he was being guarded by Cooper.

For the Celtics, Kevin McHale, the team's power forward, was 6 feet 11 inches tall, with exceptionally long arms, broad shoulders, and a powerful chest. His combination of size, strength, and finesse made him arguably the most difficult player in the league to guard. He was an excellent shooter, featuring an uncommonly soft touch and a bewildering array of moves from the low post, and he was also a tireless rebounder and a superb shot blocker. The recently

Johnson finds the going rough as he takes the ball to the hoop against Greg Kite (left) and Larry Bird (center) in Game 3 of the 1987 NBA finals. The Boston Celtics' tactic of giving a hard foul to every Los Angeles player who tried to lay the ball up or dunk it had bullied the Lakers in both the 1984 and 1985 championships— but not in their 1987 series.

concluded regular season had been the best of his outstanding career, but he was now playing with broken bones in his right ankle and foot, and the injuries greatly hampered his mobility.

Abdul-Jabbar's Boston counterpart at center was the stately Robert Parish. In these years of Abdul-Jabbar's decline, the stoic, stonefaced Chief, as Parish was known to his teammates, was in all likelihood the best all-around center in the league. His game had no real weaknesses: he was a fine scorer who tallied many of his baskets on a high-arcing turn-around jump shot; an excellent rebounder; and a good defender, one of the few who could disrupt Abdul-Jabbar. The 33-year-old Parish was also a superbly conditioned athlete, and he attempted to use his advantage in years to tire Abdul-Jabbar by beating him up and down the floor.

The man who handled the ball for the Celtics was Dennis ("D.J.") Johnson. His forte was defense, and he was charged with the uninviting task of guarding his namesake in the purple-and-gold Los Angeles uniform. On his own end of the floor, the Boston point guard was a careful, reliable ball handler and an inventive passer. The weakest part of his game was shooting. When the Lakers doubleteamed one of the Celtics, it was Johnson they were most likely to leave open and risk having score on them. That tactic often backfired in the tension-filled closing moments of games, however, when he transformed himself into one of the sport's great clutch performers. Bird considered D.J. the best ballplayer he had ever played with.

Danny Ainge, the shooting guard for the Celtics, was one of the top three-point shooters in the league. The youthful-looking Ainge had played major league baseball before making the NBA his career, and his game had benefited from his decision to concentrate on one sport. Though he was the least heralded of the Celtics starters, he had improved each year he was in the NBA, and he had a knack for playing his best in the most important games. In tight contests, Ainge's baskets were often the backbreakers; opponents concentrated on stopping his celebrated teammates, only to fall victim to the baby-faced assassin.

And then there were Larry Bird and Magic Johnson, the game's two best players. Bird was three years older than Johnson, even though they had entered the league in the same year—1979—after storied college careers that culminated in a contest between their respective universities, Indiana State and Michigan State, for the collegiate basketball championship. The immense popularity already enjoyed by the two players helped that contest become the highest-rated television broadcast of a basketball

game in history. The highest-rated basketball broad-
casts since had all been matchups of Bird's Celtics
and Magic's Lakers.

Each of these two ballplayers excelled at every
facet of the game and was a giant at his position. At
6 foot 10 inches, Bird was the Celtics small forward;
at 6 foot 9 inches, Johnson was the Lakers point
guard, a position usually reserved for individuals any-
where from six inches to a foot smaller in height. Bird
was the better shooter and scorer; Johnson, the better
ball handler. Bird always led his team in scoring and
assists, and often in rebounds as well; Magic usually
led the league in assists. In the regular season just
completed, Johnson had also led the Lakers in scoring for the first time, and he was an outstanding
rebounder. The pairing of size with passing and
shooting skills usually seen only in much smaller
players made both Bird and Magic extraordinary and
unique players.

Both men brought to the floor a creative, intui-
tive flair informed by a bedrock understanding of
the game's fundamentals. They possessed a singular
ability to see order in the swirling chaos of 10 huge,
phenomenally strong and quick men fighting each
other for position on a relatively small area of hardwood floor. And they were able to deliver the ball to
one of their teammates the instant he broke free of
his hardworking defender.

Bird was one of the greatest scorers ever to play
professional basketball. Johnson's shooting could be
criticized only in comparison to the other aspects of
his exquisite offensive game. But despite the magnificent shot-making abilities of both superstars, the
essence of their play was passing; each man looked
first to set up a teammate for a score before looking
to score himself. And the way they passed was
astounding! Look-aways, full-court bounce passes,
behind-the-back dishes, soft touch passes, pick-and-

rolls—their assists elicited roars from the capacity crowds that packed NBA arenas across the nation.

Bird and Johnson rarely did anything on the court strictly for show, however; the rousing creativity the two men brought to the floor was always in the service of getting their team an easy basket. Other players were faster, stronger, better jumpers, and sometimes more spectacular. (Neither the Boston nor the Los Angeles superstar was a master of the flamboyant dunk shots that were the greatest crowd pleasers.) But no other players were more satisfying to watch. Bird and Magic understood that the most important statistic in basketball is which team wins. No one did as much to make his team the best.

In their eighth year in the NBA, each player had come to recognize that he had only the other as the standard against which to measure his own excellence. "Larry Bird is the only player I fear," Johnson said on more than one occasion. "Magic is the only player who understands the game the way I do," Bird said. Their mutual admiration had grown over time to a friendship so close that Johnson likened it to a marriage, and they had begun to talk of retiring at the same time at some point in the future, unable to imagine finding another challenge equal to what they and their teams posed to one another.

"We're going to play the Lakers, we're going to play the Lakers," startled Celtic teammates heard the usually reserved but plainly delighted Bird chirping in a little boy's singsong cadence in the locker room several hours before a game with their archrivals. "It doesn't matter whether we're playing inside Boston Garden, with all those championship banners swinging from the sky," wrote Johnson in his 1989 book *Magic's Touch*, "that rickety old parquet floor with all its dead spots, and all those leprechaun ghosts sitting on the opponent's backboard; or if we're at the Forum with the stretch limousines and all the Hollywood stars—Jack Nicholson, O. J. Simpson, Dyan Cannon, Billy Crystal, Arsenio Hall, the Jacksons—sitting at courtside. We can have Dancing Barry rolling out of the stands and the best cheerleaders in basketball, the Laker Girls, making the whole joint crazy during every time-out, or we could be on a playground in the middle of nowhere. Whenever we play the Celtics, it seems like we're playing in the last game that'll be played in basketball history."

And to the delight of the more than 16,000 fans in the Boston Garden and the infinitely larger national television audience, Game 4 of the 1987 NBA championship finals was indeed contested as if it were the last game these or any two teams would ever play. Since Bird had joined the Celtics and Magic the Lakers, their respective clubs had each captured three NBA championships, with each team defeating the other once in the finals. To the winner of their third meeting would go the sporting press's "Team of the 1980s" title.

Most analysts and pundits favored the Lakers, even though the Celtics were seeking to defend their crown and become the NBA's first repeat champion in 18 years. During the regular season, Los Angeles had won more games than any team in the league. The Lakers were younger, faster, and had a deeper bench than the Celtics did. And they had Magic Johnson playing at a higher level than he had at any point in his storied career.

With Abdul-Jabbar finally showing some of the effects of his advanced athletic age, Pat Riley, the Lakers coach, had asked Johnson to elevate his already exalted game a notch. For the first time in his career, he was called upon to be Los Angeles's leading scorer. Magic, who had never before averaged over 20 points a game for a season, responded by averaging a career-high 24 points a game. Those numbers silenced the critics who had charged that,

A Magic moment follows the Los Angeles Lakers' triumph over the Boston Celtics in Game 6 to clinch the 1987 NBA championship: Johnson (right) is mobbed by fans at the Los Angeles Forum.

for all his greatness, he was not an especially good shooter. Meanwhile, he continued his sterling passing: his average of 12 assists per game led the league.

Johnson's overall play in 1987 earned him his first NBA Most Valuable Player Award. But he still awaited the opportunity to atone for the one great failing of his professional career: his uncharacteristic miscues in the tense closing moments of several of the games of the 1984 championship series had helped deny the Lakers the crown. Those failures were cited often by those who regarded Bird, who had already won three Most Valuable Player Awards, as the superior player.

The Lakers entered the 1987 finals loose and confident. "There's no question this is the best team I've played on," Johnson said. "It's fast, it can shoot and rebound, it has inside people, it has everything.

I've never played on a team that had everything before."

Judging by the results of the first two games of the best-of-seven series, the Celtics had never played *against* a team that had everything before. With Johnson running the Lakers' famed fast break in front of the fans and film stars at the Forum in Los Angeles, the Lakers won both contests easily, 126–113 and 141–122. Incredibly, the defending champions looked old and tired, as if they did not even belong on the same court as Los Angeles. Performing with stunning speed and precision, the Lakers dominated the boards and gathered every loose ball, while a relentless Magic ran the team's carefully orchestrated offense to perfection, foiling every strategy Boston had devised to slow him down. In the first half of the first game, Los Angeles ran its fast break an incredible 35 times in 45 possessions. It was a devastating demonstration of the high-energy, high-speed Laker style known as Showtime.

But the Celtics were too savvy, too proud, and too good to quit. Bird put the needle to his teammates for their shabby performance on the road. "If this continues," he said, "maybe it's time to make some changes and get some people who will play hard every night and not just in front of their families." He went on to say that the Celtics needed "twelve heart transplants." As always, his teammates responded to their leader's cajoling.

The return to Boston Garden, where they had won a league-record 48 consecutive games over 1986 and 1987, also seemed to rejuvenate the Celtics. In Game 3, they succeeded for the first time in slowing down Johnson and the Lakers. Playing the controlled half-court style that they preferred, which depended on careful ball handling, excellent shooting, superior rebounding, and the canny exploitation of mismatches in the low post rather than the use of speed and quickness, the Celtics rode Bird's 30 points to a 109–103 victory.

The Boston victory made Game 4 crucial for both teams. The Celtics' tremendous success at home over the past two seasons left them confident that they could take the next two games, both of which would be played in Boston, and return to Los Angeles needing to win just one of the series' final two contests to claim the title. Two more Celtics victories at home would also mean that for the Lakers to win, the series would have to go to seven games, and Los Angeles had never won a seventh game against Boston in six tries.

With the cries of the roaring faithful shaking Boston Garden, the Celtics came out smoking in Game 4. For the second straight game, the bigger Celtics succeeded in controlling the pace, dominating the boards, and preventing the speedier Lakers from kicking their fast break into gear. By the midpoint of the third quarter, Boston held a commanding 79–63 lead, and it seemed clear that the series was turning in the Celtics' favor. Now it was the Lakers who seemed overwhelmed and tentative, their finesse no match for the more physical style of the Celtics.

In the television booths and the press box, sports journalists were reviving old criticisms: that the Lakers' considerable flash masked an essential lack of substance; that if you took away their fast break, they were unwilling to pay the price, in terms of the less glamorous hard work of defense and rebounding necessary to win; that they were truly a Hollywood team, all glitz but little fiber; that they could be physically intimidated; that they could be forced into mistakes at crucial moments.

On the floor, the Celtics resorted to the same tactics that had helped them beat Los Angeles for the championship in 1984. Any Laker who beat his man on a drive to the basket was fouled, extremely hard,

Lakers coach Pat Riley is doused with champagne in the clubhouse following Game 6 of the 1987 NBA championship. "Looking back, I'd have to say that the 1986–87 season was the most fun I'd ever had," Magic said. "I had my best overall season in the NBA."

before he could lay the ball up or dunk it. The cost to the Celtics was two foul shots; the hope was that the Lakers would think twice about taking the ball to the hoop.

This strategy had left the Lakers admittedly cowed in 1984, but they were now a more mature team. When Greg Kite, the Celtics hatchet man, began throwing his weight around, the usually imperturbable Worthy took exception, and a brief scuffle occurred. After that, the Lakers began to dig in and fight back. The hard work that fueled the Lakers' style of play had often been overlooked by those who saw only the glamour and grace. Yet the intense, hard-driving Riley had always preached the virtues of rebounding and defense to his charges. His formula was simple: "No rebounds, no rings," he often said, referring to the gaudy baubles with which the NBA rewarded all the members of the championship team. His logic was inarguable, for to run the fast break effectively, a team needs to force its opponents to mishandle the ball or miss shots, then gather the rebounds that begin the headlong dash to the other end of the floor.

By the time both teams took the floor for the fourth quarter—the 12-minute portion of the game that Johnson refers to simply as "winning time"—the Lakers had whittled into the Celtics' lead. Spurred on by Magic, Los Angeles had begun to play better defense than any observer could recall, and the Celtics were finding it extremely hard to get good shots, even though the game was being played at the tempo they preferred. Each possession became a war, with the players hounding one another and jousting doggedly for position.

There remained very few high-flying, carefree forays to the hoop by Los Angeles. But Magic, as he did better than anyone else, was finding the open man. And as the overworked Celtics starting five—having no one on the bench of the caliber of the Lakers' Cooper and Mychal Thompson, a talented forward and center, Boston was reluctant to substitute—began to tire, the Lakers at last drew even.

NBA games, however, tend to progress in ebbs and flows. The Lakers became somewhat wearied by the effort expended in trimming the deficit, and the canny Celtics regrouped and ran their lead back up to eight points with just two minutes left to play. It was a seemingly safe margin in the hands of such a tested bunch of veterans.

To the disbelief of the overwrought Boston crowd, the Lakers came back again. And with 34 seconds left to play, they took the lead, 104–103, for the first time all game. Then, with Cooper stalking him, Bird demonstrated the kind of last-second heroics that had earned him the simple nickname "the Legend" by nailing a three-point shot from deep along the left baseline.

With the crowd in a frenzy, Los Angeles raced the ball upcourt and missed a hurried shot; the Celtics rebounded. Ahead by two points and with a chance to secure the win, Boston ran its pet play, Thumb-down. It called for Bird to free himself from the tenacious Cooper by curling around screens set by his teammates and come from the baseline to the area of the foul line, where he would receive the ball, with the option to shoot it or pass it down low to McHale.

The play seemed unstoppable. But Magic, who had spent countless hours studying films of the Celtics in action, foresaw what was coming and left his own man unguarded. In the instant that McHale flashed open, Bird sent him the basketball in the form of a touch pass, instantaneously redirecting the ball when it reached him as he came to the key. Bird's pass was a masterpiece of split-second timing, vision, improvisation, anticipation, and preparation, but so was Magic's reaction. Darting from his own man, he managed to deflect Bird's pass just enough so that it arrived near McHale's feet, the very last place one wants to throw a basketball to a hobbling 6-foot-11-inch man. The ball bounced off McHale's leg and rolled out of bounds. Laker ball.

A foul shot by Abdul-Jabbar cut the lead to one. His second free throw missed, but the rebound, fiercely contested by McHale and Thompson, again went out of bounds off the Celtics player. There were eight seconds remaining.

As the Lakers and Celtics huddled around their coaches, plotting their final strategy, the stunned crowd looked on in near silence, unable to believe that the misfortunes that usually befell opponents in this allegedly haunted arena were being visited on their own heroes.

The two teams broke from their huddles. Worthy inbounded the ball from near center court. In the welter of straining bodies near the basket, Dennis Johnson was screened off his man, and Magic emerged alone to take the ball, about 20 feet from the basket, on the left side of the court. The game

Johnson is all smiles as he clutches the Maurice Podoloff Trophy in recognition of being named the most valuable player of the 1986-87 NBA season; he became only the third guard in league history to receive the award, which he won again in 1988-89 and 1989-90. His other achievements include being honored as playoff MVP in 1980, 1982, and 1987 and All-Star Game MVP in 1990 and 1992.

clock soundlessly ticked, and the amber lights flashed down to seven.

Johnson's first instinct was to take a jump shot from the spot where he was standing. But there was long-armed Kevin McHale racing toward him, faster than the forward's gimpy leg should have allowed. For an instant, the two faced off: McHale, crouched in his defender's stance, arms waving; Johnson, also bent at the waist and knees, torso and head thrust forward, right foot ahead, toeing the hardwood meaningfully, testing McHale's response, with the ball held protectively at his right side. For a lesser instant he thought of passing inside to Abdul-Jabbar, but the big man was covered by Parish. The scoreboard clock changed to six.

"I knew I could get around Kevin," Magic said later, "but I didn't know what I would do when I did. So I started to drive."

Pounding the ball against the hardwood in his trademark high dribble, Johnson drove right, into and across the foul lane as the clock blinked to five and McHale scuttled frantically to his left in a vain attempt to keep pace. But the Celtic defender, outdistanced by just the portion of a step that would allow Johnson to launch his shot, had help. As the shot clock showed four, Parish left his man to switch to Magic and blocked the Laker guard's intended route to the basket. So Johnson continued right, across the lane just below the foul line, as the seconds dwindled to three.

With the towering Parish and McHale dogging his footsteps, Johnson pivoted on his left foot and launched the basketball, in conscious emulation of Abdul-Jabbar, whose signature skyhook shot he had been practicing all season but had not yet dared unveil; Magic termed his own version of the shot a "junior, junior, junior skyhook." The ball arched teasingly above the reaching fingers of the two taller men in the white-and-green Boston jerseys and floated tantalizingly toward the hoop before passing softly through the rim and cords and bouncing away beneath the basket. A great moan of anguish escaped the Boston crowd as each of the five Celtics players reflexively brought his hands together to signal for a time-out. The amber lights read two.

When play resumed, Bird managed to get off a desperation three-pointer. The ball bounded harmlessly off the back iron, and the final buzzer sounded with Los Angeles clinging to a 107–106 advantage. Secure with their three-games-to-one lead, Magic and the Lakers nailed down their fourth championship of the decade back in Los Angeles.

At the press conference following the series finale, a disappointed but appreciative Bird mustered a rueful smile. Then, speaking in his soft Indiana twang, he expressed what had been made apparent to the rest of the basketball world. "Magic's the best," Bird said. "He's the best I've ever seen. He's a perfect basketball player." ☙

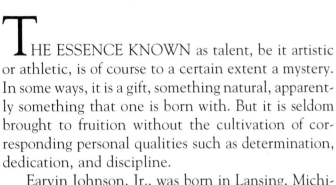

2

TIP-OFF

T HE ESSENCE KNOWN as talent, be it artistic or athletic, is of course to a certain extent a mystery. In some ways, it is a gift, something natural, apparently something that one is born with. But it is seldom brought to fruition without the cultivation of corresponding personal qualities such as determination, dedication, and discipline.

Earvin Johnson, Jr., was born in Lansing, Michigan, on August 14, 1959. He was the fourth of Earvin and Christine Johnson's seven children. The family lived in a two-story yellow frame house on Middle Street, which is, as its name suggests, in the heart of the city.

Lansing, situated in the center of Michigan, is the state capital. Yet the city's economic well-being since World War II has depended upon the automobile industry, with the manufacturers of cars and car parts employing many more people than the state government. In the 1960s, when Earvin Johnson, Jr., was

The future basketball great grew up in this yellow frame house at 814 Middle Street in Lansing, Michigan. "Nine of us, sometimes ten, lived there," Johnson recalled. "My mother and father had the big bedroom. Quincy, Larry, and I had another, and the four girls, Lily Pearl, Kim, and the twins, Evelyn and Yvonne, shared the third."

A beaming Earvin, Jr., the middle child in Earvin, Sr., and Christine Johnson's large and closely knit family. "The strength comes from my father, the smile from my mother," Magic said. "People talk about my smile, but hers is the original."

growing up, the American automobile industry had not yet been hard hit by foreign competition, and Lansing enjoyed a period of relative prosperity.

Boasting a population of more than 100,000, the city suffered from some of the same problems—such as crime, poverty, and drug abuse—that can be found in any urban area. But these economic and social ills were not nearly as significant as those that, for example, beset Detroit, located 90 miles to the east. The state's largest city, with a population more than 10 times as large as Lansing's, Detroit experienced riots in the summer of 1967 that destroyed much of its inner city; federal troops had to be summoned to restore order. Lansing knew no such civil unrest.

The Johnsons lived in a lower-middle-class neighborhood of two-story frame houses much like their own. Most families owned their homes. Most of the men worked in either the automobile or the construction industries.

Like Earvin and Christine Johnson, many of the black men and women living in Lansing had been born and raised in the South and had come north shortly after World War II, a time when a large number of southern blacks left their homes in search of greater economic opportunity. The war and the enormous prosperity that followed it resulted in a huge expansion of the United States's industrial capacity. Manpower was needed to keep America's factories and plants humming around the clock.

For many southern blacks, the relatively well-paying industrial jobs in the North represented a significantly better opportunity for economic advancement than anything available to them in the overwhelmingly agricultural South. The great northward migration of southern blacks that resulted from such limited economic opportunity and the overt racial oppression of the South soon transformed such midwestern cities as Chicago, Detroit, Gary, and Lansing.

Earvin Johnson, Sr., came to Lansing from Wesson, Mississippi, where his family toiled as sharecroppers. "At the time, I always thought we got half of what we produced for working the land," he recalled. "That's how it was supposed to work. But looking back, I realized we never got what we earned."

The move north to Lansing did not mean an end to all hardship. To support his 10 children, Magic's father always worked at least two jobs. (Three of those children, for whom the senior Johnson maintained financial responsibility, were from a marriage preceding his one to Christine.)

Earvin, Sr.'s primary employment was with the Fisher Body Corporation, a manufacturer of Oldsmobile bodies. Initially, he worked the grinding boot on the 4:00 P.M. to 1:00 A.M. shift. The grinding boot was a machine for smoothing out metal; when the Big E, as he was known to his children, returned home to Middle Street in the early-morning hours, his clothes and even his skin were often pockmarked with burns from the sparks thrown off by the boot. After he had built up sufficient seniority, Johnson transferred to the position of intermediate relief man, which meant that he filled in where needed on the assembly line. He continued to work the same grueling late-night hours, however.

For several years, Johnson pumped gas during the daytime at a filling station. He eventually saved enough money to buy a secondhand truck, with which he started a cleaning business. After finishing the evening shift at Fisher, he would clean out offices, shops, and stores for several hours, head home to grab a little sleep, then spend the hours between nine in the morning and the start of a new shift hauling and carting with the truck.

"I'd like to say it was like death," Earvin, Jr., remembered his father saying to him once about this backbreaking schedule, "but I've never seen death, so maybe this was worse." The comment was simply an acknowledgment of difficulty, not a complaint. "No one told me to have 10 children; I had a choice, you know," Earvin, Sr., often said in attempting to instill in his children a lesson about responsibility—a lesson about which his actions spoke far louder than his words.

Magic's mother, Christine, also worked two jobs: her eight-hour-a-day position as a school custodian, and the full-time task of raising her brood. By all accounts, she is an exceptionally warm and gracious woman, with a huge smile "as bright as the sun at midday," in the words of her fourth child. Relatives and childhood friends of Magic Johnson know that he inherited his celebrated smile from his mother.

Because Earvin, Sr., was usually at work, Christine was the more constant presence in the house. According to her most famous child, who was called Junior, she "handled the day-to-day traumas of family life . . . arbitrated arguments over bathroom rights, gave out the punishments for missed chores, and generally kept seven children in line." When the occasional unruliness of her charges threatened to overwhelm her, she had an infallible, if hardly unique, measure for restoring order: the threat of informing their father of their transgressions. No one in the Johnson household wanted to be responsible for upsetting the Big E during his few restful hours at home.

There was seldom need to resort to such drastic measures. None of the Johnson children ever got into serious trouble; maintaining order in the house usually required little more than refereeing sibling squabbles or keeping track of the whereabouts of each of the children. Usually a holler out the front door was

sufficient to accomplish the latter, for Middle Street was filled dawn to dusk with children playing kickball, tag, football, and hide-and-seek. Magic remembered the street being quiet only after dark, by which time all the children had been called inside.

When the Johnson children were tuckered out at last, they tumbled into bed in two bedrooms upstairs. The four girls—Lily Pearl, Kim, and the twins Evelyn and Yvonne—shared one room; the three boys—Quincy, Larry, and Junior—shared the other. On Sundays, the seven children were rousted early from their sleep, washed, and dressed in their best clothes, for Christine and Earvin Johnson were serious churchgoers. All their children took part in the services, either as ushers or members of the choir.

All in all, the Johnsons seem to have constituted that most enviable of human relationships: a genuinely happy family. Certainly there were day-to-day sorrows and worries. Their jobs and family responsibilities left Earvin, Sr., and Christine constantly fatigued; the younger Earvin remembered coming home from school to find his exhausted mother asleep in a chair at the dining-room table, in the midst of preparing dinner, her head propped up in her hand. Both parents worried constantly about having enough money to keep their children well fed and well clothed. Yet there was usually enough; young Earvin even had a bicycle, which he rarely used because none of the other kids in the neighborhood had one, and he had no one to ride with.

Christine, who was from a rural community in the tobacco country of North Carolina, sometimes lamented that her children had never known the unhurried pleasantries of country life. She also loved to reminisce to her sons and daughters about the times when her whole family would go together to watch the town baseball team, on which her father was a star second baseman and outfielder, play against a neighboring community. "All the families came out," she told her children. "It was a big party, and they'd set up these big old barrels of lemonade for all the kids."

There was one game that Christine remembered especially well, for it was the occasion of her meeting a tall, skinny, shy young serviceman named Earvin Johnson. "He looked so lonesome standing there by himself," she remembered. "I felt sorry for him, so I asked him how he was doing and things like that."

Christine would always end her recollections the same way: "Yep, you kids today don't know what you missed." But whatever regrets or worries she and her husband might have had were easily outweighed by the joys of the life they shared together with their family. Weekends were always special; on Saturday night, Earvin, Sr., often took the boys to watch drag races at a nearby strip, and on Sunday the family had a rare opportunity to eat together. Christine's cooking was legendary in the neighborhood. Many years later, the Los Angeles Lakers would consider their once-a-year trip to Detroit one of the highlights of the season, for it meant that their locker room would be filled with superb down-home cuisine prepared by Magic's mother.

Earvin, Jr., developed his interest in basketball by the time he was about to enter the third grade. That summer, June Bug, a nickname bestowed on the younger Earvin by his father, began to disappear. He would be gone from the house before his parents awoke, and he rarely returned before nightfall. Even on Sundays, he would be up, dressed, and out of the house long before his mother came in to to wake him for church. When school started in the fall, he usually awoke and left the house hours before classes started. At first his parents were worried, but the mystery was soon solved: Junior was spending virtually every waking minute on one of the four basketball courts outside the school at West and Main streets, two blocks from his house.

"When Earvin first started getting up and going to play early, we wondered where he was," his mother recalled. "I finally had to tell him not ever to leave home without ever telling us where he was going. After that he would always wake me up around daybreak to tell me he was going up to the courts."

Pat Riley liked to joke that "Magic came out of the womb passing the basketball." But Earvin's basketball development was not quite that rapid. Like any beginner, he struggled at first, and he would remember feeling tremendously awkward on the court, so much so that his older brother Larry, another habitué of the Main Street courts, was not especially eager to let this clumsy little tagalong into the games that he and his friends played.

Young Earvin was tireless, however, and his enthusiasm for the game was boundless. He learned quickly, from whomever was willing to teach him. His father, a longtime basketball fan who recognized that there might be something special in his son's passion for the game, put up a rim and backboard in the driveway. And in the little free time that he had, he and his son shot hoops together.

"Dave Bing was always my favorite player," Johnson said of the all-star guard (far left) who guided the Detroit Pistons from 1966 to 1975. Magic discovered what he called "the simple secrets of basketball" by observing on television how Bing and other top professionals played the game.

The Big E was a stickler for fundamentals. He made the right-handed Junior learn to shoot and dribble with his left hand as well. Earvin, Sr.'s constant lesson was that in basketball one must be a complete player. It is not enough to be just a good shooter, or a good rebounder, or a good dribbler, he said.

"My dad taught me never to be satisfied with just one aspect of my game," Magic stated in *Magic's Touch*. "He said I had to learn to do *everything* at least well. Not perfect, but well enough to be able to rely on any skill whenever I needed it. I had to be able to shoot so that I'd have confidence taking the big shot at the end of the game. I had to learn to block out and rebound so that I could help my teammates on the boards. I had to be able to play defense so that I could stop my man down the stretch. I had to be able to dribble with both hands and my head up so that I could get around pressure defenses. I had to be able to make every kind of pass imaginable so I could get the ball to an open teammate in any situation. But most important, I had to understand the concepts of the game so that I could make the right decisions. I had to learn all of that before I could come in off the driveway."

When the outdoor lessons were concluded, the indoor sessions began. On weekends during the NBA season, father and son would watch ballgames on television, especially those of the Detroit Pistons. Longtime doormats in the NBA, the Pistons were then edging toward respectability as a result of the inspired play of their new star, Dave Bing. The thin, high-scoring guard was a marvel. Every player on the Main Street courts wanted to emulate his springy, picture-perfect jump shot.

The Big E pointed out to his son that playing good basketball "was more than just watching NBA players on television and trying to copy them without any thought, preparation, practice, or concept of the fundamentals." As they watched, he explained to the receptive boy the little things on the basketball court that often go unnoticed by the casual observer but that often make the difference between winning and losing: the way a player moves without the ball, when and why a player leaves his own man to help out on defense, what constitutes a mismatch and how to take advantage of one.

"Watching Dave Bing and his teammates with my father was how I learned the simple secrets of basketball," Magic recalled. "Dad pointed out everything down to the smallest detail—the footwork, the head fakes, the defensive stances, blocking out underneath the boards, things that separated the great players

A ball-handling wizard who bore the nickname Magic long before Earvin did, Earl Monroe was another of the NBA guards whose moves and tactics Johnson studied and admired. The youngster eventually incorporated Monroe's trademark spin dribble into his own "hoopsy-doopsy," fast-breaking style of play.

from the good players. . . . My father would point out things to me as we watched, things like a big guard taking a smaller guard underneath, or guys running a pick-and-roll."

There were limits on the Big E's time, however, and his son's passion for the game quickly exhausted the energies his father had left at the end of his long workdays. So the majority of young Earvin's most valuable basketball lessons came in the schoolyard. There he tried to put into practice what his father had taught him.

Competition at the Main Street schoolyard was tough. Players came from around Lansing to test their reputations, often in front of small crowds of critical, vocal onlookers attracted by the park's reputation for featuring the city's best playground competition. There were only four courts at Main Street, and only the best players got to play. The usual playground rules prevailed: the winning team stayed on the court for another game; the losers walked. A team kept the court as long as it kept winning—all day long, if it was good enough.

These rules were fine with young Earvin. At first, he found it difficult to get court time. The older kids dominated the courts; the only way Earvin and his friends could get to play was to show up very early in the morning, before anyone else was there, or to scramble on for some quick action while the older boys were taking a rest.

The youngster soon discovered that if he hung around long enough, he could get in some games. In the winter, when snow drove many of the kids indoors, he even shoveled off the courts so that he could play. By the time he reached the fourth and fifth grades, he was better than any child his age in the organized school and recreational leagues in which he had begun to take part. He was so good, in fact, that he sometimes scored all of his team's points in a game.

And he was growing. When Earvin entered the seventh grade, he stood 6 feet tall. Two years later, he was 6 feet 5. His height allowed him to get into games at Main Street with boys older and better at basketball than he was, which was a surefire way to improve his game in a hurry.

It was around this time that Earvin learned how to keep his usually older and often demanding team-mates happy: pass them the basketball. Young hoop-sters generally regard scoring as the most important part of basketball, and in schoolyard games the emphasis is often on one-on-one play, in which a player always looks to score when the ball comes to

him, rather than on teamwork. An unselfish player—
one who looks first to set up his teammate for a basket
with a clever pass—is a rare commodity and usually
a highly desired teammate. Other players always love
to team up with someone who is willing and able to
pass them the basketball when and where they want
it. And Earvin had learned early from his father a
lesson that even many NBA players fail to com-
prehend: to win, a team must play unselfishly.

Soon, Earvin had no trouble getting into games;
and once he got on the court, he seldom left it, for
his teams rarely lost. Even though he was not an
especially good outside shooter—to his eternal disappointment, he discovered that he did not have the
spring in his legs to emulate the beloved Dave Bing
jumper (Magic's somewhat awkward jump shot would
always be the least stylish element of his game)—he
found other ways to score. In Earvin's opinion, time
on the court was too valuable to risk losing a game
with untrustworthy outside shots, so he took the ball
to the hoop, relentlessly, in a fast-breaking, driving
style of play that he called "hoopsy-doopsy." Others
would later call it Showtime.

Earvin handled the ball even when, as was increasingly often the case, he was the tallest player on
the court. His teammates never minded. They knew
that the instant they flashed open, the ball would be
delivered perfectly to them. All they had to do was
make the shot.

Besides, endless practice had given Earvin the
best "handle" in Lansing. He had honed his ball-
handling skills in countless full-court one-on-one
games with his brother Larry and by dribbling a
basketball wherever he went: to school, to church,
to the movies, even in his bed at night. The *thump-
thump* of a basketball being dribbled soon became
Christine's most reliable indicator of her son's pre-

sence in the house. (She knew he had been practicing his shooting indoors when she was unable to find her other children's socks. Earvin used them, rolled up, as balls to shoot at paper bags or wastepaper baskets.)

By the time he entered high school, the tall, skinny Earvin Johnson, with his trademark red Converse Chuck Taylor All-Stars with the multicolored laces, was the acknowledged king of the Main Street courts. ❧

Tell-Star . . . DWIGH

Volume 18   April, 1974

Johnson Breaks City Recor

Earvin Johnson a six-foot five-inch ninth grader broke the city junior high school individual scoring record with 48 points in the 89-25 crushing of Otto.

Being a very versatile basketball player he scores an average of 24 points a game and has led the team in scoring for most of the regular season games.

He naturally was very happy and overwhelmed when he had been informed that he had broken the city basketball record for individual scoring.

Unfortunately, he was not awarded the game ball for this great achievement "The team and the coach has made the difference in my playing.

In the future Earvin plans to keep on playing ball up through high school college and into the proffesional ranks. He also plans to start a business and to travel.

He will be going to either Sexton or Everett High School so.........
Congratulations and good luck in your future years!

Hey, have you ever wondered about how many people went to the Dwight Rich basketball games?? Recently I took a survey and it averaged out to 10 out of 10 people going to the game. The girls I asked said the young men on both teams look nice. Some of the young men I asked said the

3

MAKING MAGIC

❧

EARVIN JOHNSON'S REPUTATION as a basketball player soon spread far beyond the confines of the Main Street courts. He was in the seventh grade at Dwight Rich Junior High School when the first newspaper article extolling his talents appeared. To his amazement, total strangers, many of them adults, soon began approaching him on the street to express their admiration for his ability.

At a local gymnasium where Johnson and his friends often went to watch Michigan State University players work out in the off-season, he was astonished to be recognized and singled out for attention by Terry Furlow, the Spartans' high-scoring guard. When Furlow asked Johnson if he wanted to join in a scrimmage—"Can you play or what?" the college star challenged—the younger player was not initially sure if he could compete successfully against college-level players. But he more than held his own.

"The first time I went up there it was just to watch," Johnson remembered of his trip to the gym. "Then Terry picked me to play with him and I was scared. But then he started calling me his main man and bragging on me. I never forgot that."

"Congratulations and good luck in your future years!" the April 1974 issue of Tell-Star, the Dwight Rich Junior High School newspaper, wishes Johnson shortly after the ninth-grader's 48 points against Otto Junior High broke Lansing's junior high school single-game scoring record. The 14-year-old wound up averaging 24 points a game for the season.

"I spent so much time on the Main Street courts that I could have had my mail delivered there," Johnson (top row, middle) recalled. "During the school year I would get up early in the morning, long before I had to, and practice before breakfast." But he had other interests as a youngster besides basketball, and playing football was among them.

The gangly teenage phenomenon promptly became a regular participant in pickup games at the gym. Among the other players were Furlow, Campanella ("Campy") Russell, and Ben Poquette—all of whom played ball at Michigan colleges and subsequently made it to the NBA—and smooth George ("the Iceman") Gervin, whose repertoire of uncanny shots had already made him a star in professional basketball.

The attention was a welcome boost to the adolescent's self-esteem. But his teachers and parents made sure that his ego remained in check. When Johnson failed to turn in a school assignment, his teacher, Greta Dart, prohibited him from playing in a championship game against a rival school. Johnson protested vehemently, but Dart stood fast, and his parents supported her. The incident even marked the start of a close friendship between the educator and the parents of the basketball star, who recognized that the teacher had their son's best interests at heart.

At about this same time, Johnson first began to talk about making a career as a professional basketball player. His mother was encouraging, but she did not take the prospect overly seriously. She knew the odds against that sort of athletic success were astronomically long. "That'll be nice, son," Christine Johnson would say when Earvin told her about the big house he was going to buy for her when he made it in the pros.

Meanwhile, Earvin's mother continued to hold out hope that he would become a minister, for she had long dreamed of having a clergyman in the family. For a time, she also thought that he might become a musician. When it became too dark to play basketball any longer, her son was fond of harmonizing with his buddies in impromptu streetcorner song sessions in the hope of impressing the young ladies in the neighborhood. Earvin had a fine voice and some musical talent; he had continued to sing in the church choir (when he did not skip services in favor of the basketball court), and he even played the electric bass for a while. But he would never devote the kind of time to music that he did to playing ball. "I loved music, but not like I loved basketball," he said later.

The graduation from Dwight Rich of the 6-foot-5-inch sensation, who was already being touted as one of the best players in the state, was awaited with eagerness and trepidation by high school basketball coaches in Lansing and elsewhere in Michigan. Only one of them would have the pleasure of coaching Johnson as he completed the 10th through 12th grades. The others would have the three-year challenge of devising strategies to stop him.

While Johnson was growing up, he had assumed that he would attend classes and play ball at Sexton, which was the high school nearest his home on Middle Street. But the federal courts in the early

1970s approved the use of busing as a means to create racially balanced student bodies in school districts where decades of discrimination in education and housing had created all-white and all-black public schools. The upshot for Johnson was that he was to be bused, along with other black youths from his neighborhood, to Everett High School, a predominantly white educational institution farther away from his home.

Earvin was not especially pleased with the notion. His brother Quincy had been among the first group of black students to be bused to Everett, and their arrival in the previously segregated neighborhood triggered demonstrations by the white residents. The buses were often pelted with bottles, stones, and bricks as they arrived at the school in the morning. Protesters chanted racial epithets at the students as they disembarked. Within the school, there were frequent fights between white and black students.

By the time Earvin's older brother Larry began attending Everett, the more overt nastiness had died down. But he still found it an unpleasant environment. To make matters worse, Larry was cut from the school's basketball team, the Vikings, and he thought his release might have been racially motivated. The team's longtime coach, George Fox, was unused to dealing with black players, and he was not much interested in learning, Larry believed. When it came time for Earvin to go to Everett, Larry did not even want his heralded younger brother to try out for the school team.

Earvin, who did not want to attend Everett, resolved to make the best of his situation. He did not have much choice. He had filed a petition of protest with the school board to let him attend Sexton, but his request was denied. His parents advised him that if he wanted to play high school ball, he was going to have to play for Fox.

Even though Earvin was not initially enamored of Fox or the style of basketball he favored, the coach was thrilled to have a player of Johnson's caliber come along. "Just wait," Fox told some of the other coaches in Everett's conference after watching an awesome Johnson performance in a summer-league game prior to his official enrollment at the high school. "I got a kid here who's going to make believers out of everybody."

Yet their initial relationship was rocky, for Fox was a coach from the old school. His understanding of basketball fundamentals failed to take into account the way the game had changed—and was still changing—in large part because of the creativity brought to it by black athletes. He believed in an extremely disciplined, controlled brand of basketball. Plays were called from the bench on virtually every offensive possession, and the players were expected to execute them to perfection. No latitude was allowed for improvisation.

Johnson would later characterize Fox as a typical "product of the small-town Midwest: religious, hard-working, honest, a man of strong will and principles." But, the ballplayer hastened to add, "neither success nor blacks had played a part in his modest career."

Fox was not unlike a generation of white coaches who were unprepared for the way the game had evolved. The talents and innovations of players such as Earvin Johnson outraced these coaches' conception of the game, and they responded with bewilderment and, in some cases, condemnation, a not unusual response to innovation in any field of endeavor. The newer style of basketball owed much more to spontaneity and sheer athleticism, in the form of speed and jumping ability, than did the old. Hidebound coaches criticized it as undisciplined and needlessly flashy.

Over time, however, acceptance inevitably took place. A case in point is the dunk shot. Initially, coaches condemned it as hotdogging and championed instead the more traditional method of banking the ball gently against the glass when the shooter was in close to the basket.

Then came along a legion of high-flying, predominantly black players who paraded their skills as aerialists. Among them were the New York City playground legends Connie Hawkins and Earl ("the Goat") Manigault, who inspired and gave way to Julius ("Dr. J") Erving, whose feats were in turn emulated by the sport's preeminent flier, Michael Jordan. When these and other players showed that they were capable of elevating from as far as 15 feet away from the basket, soaring over their earthbound colleagues, and stuffing the ball downward through the rim, coaches were forced to reconsider their own position on the dunk.

Today, the dunk is regarded as fundamental to the game. Coaches have been forced to recognize that with skilled players performing the dunk, it is a much harder shot to block than a lay-up. Players are urged to "take the ball to the rack with authority"—drive hard to the basket and dunk the ball. Largely because of the skill of black players, it is now commonplace for the sport to be played "above the rim."

But the game as Fox understood it was not. Neither was basketball as Johnson played it. He had never been a very good jumper. His game was characterized by other nuances and flourishes that were equally baffling to his new coach. Johnson was already fundamentally sound enough to be effective playing any style, but he was at his best in the running game, where his singular ball-handling skills, his "hoopsy-doopsy" determination to drive to the basket, his unique ability to deliver the ball to the open man, and his unerring instinct for making split-second decisions in the midst of the free-flowing spontaneity on the court could best be utilized.

Fox had never been a devotee of the running game, and he disapproved of some of the means—behind-the-back dribbles and passes, no-look feeds—that his new star employed to achieve the admittedly desirable end of getting his team a basket. To Fox, such moves were flashy and unnecessary, a form of showboating. And so it took him some time to see that in the hands of as skilled and practiced a player as Johnson, such moves were as fundamental as more time-honored methods. The behind-the-back dribble, for example, allows the ball handler to change directions while interposing his body between the defender and the ball. The look-away and behind-the-back passes serve to deceive the defender as to the direction in which the basketball is to be passed.

Above all, Fox was a stickler for the old basketball saying that the ball handler should never leave the floor—that is, jump in the air, as if to shoot or pass—without knowing exactly whether and how he intends to shoot or pass. The adage is essentially a sound one. There is only a split second in which to make a choice; and an undecided player usually either makes a bad pass, takes a bad shot, or gets called for a traveling violation.

But this maxim fails to take into account players as heady and creative as Johnson, who would often intentionally leave his feet without knowing for certain what he was going to do with the ball, confident in his ability to improvise a solution that would create a basket. Johnson always used such moves for a purpose, not for show. They served to reveal his deeper understanding of the game rather than any disregard for its fundamentals, just as a talented jazz soloist's improvisation on a well-known

By the time Johnson entered the seventh grade, he was "much bigger than kids my age, a good ball handler, and an expert shooter," he recalled. "I stood six-even when I started Dwight Rich Junior High, six foot four the next year, and six-five as a ninth grader."

tune reveals a deeper understanding of the music's essence and possibilities rather than a disrespect for the original composition.

To Fox's credit, he quickly recognized that to shackle Johnson's game would be counterproductive, and the coach loosened up quite a bit. In truth, his initial bewilderment with Johnson was understandable, for even later on, among the pros of the NBA, the absolute best basketball players in the world, Johnson's skills would make him unique and cause no small amount of confusion. No player of his size had ever handled the ball so well.

This combination of natural attributes and carefully honed ability enabled Johnson to add a new variation on the fast break. Because he was so tall, he often rebounded the ball himself. And because he was such a superb ball handler, he often raced the ball the length of the floor, eschewing the outlet pass and freeing his teammates to sprint to a spot on the floor from where they could score. The fast break usually culminated with a spectacular assist from Johnson or an easy basket by him. On the high school level, his combination of size and skills made him an absolute phenomenon.

By the time the season started, the coach and the sophomore wunderkind had reached a better understanding of one another. Stunned by Johnson's performance in practices, Fox had come to realize that the teenager possessed the vision, intelligence, and basketball sophistication to create in a few seconds of flash and daring what less skilled players had often required more than a minute of careful passing and dribbling to find: a good shot. And Johnson had come to see that his coach was essentially a good man, somewhat set in his conservative ways but willing to learn and grow.

"All he really requested was dedication," Johnson said of Fox many years later. "His saying was, 'If you want to be a ballplayer, you have to work; if you don't, hit the road.'"

On this matter, at least, both coach and player were traditionalists. "To me," Johnson said, "there's only one way to think about this game and one way to play it. That's all out, foot to the floor, pushing myself as hard as I can as long as I can." And so he practiced harder and longer than anyone else.

Despite the growth in understanding between Johnson and Fox, it took some time for the Vikings to jell. The squad had won the league title the previous year, and some of the returning upperclassmen, most of whom were white, were jealous of the attention paid to Johnson, who was being touted for all-state honors before he had even played a high school game. Matters came to a head at a practice before the season began. Several times, a wide-open Johnson was ignored by one of the team's white seniors, who fired up wild shots instead of passing him the ball. This was an affront to Johnson's basketball sensibilities, but he was willing to concede that his teammate might not possess the same vision and court awareness that he did.

Subsequent observation indicated that the senior did not seem to have the same difficulty when the open man was a friend and upperclassman. When the oversight happened again, Johnson exploded. "Give it up," he screamed at his teammate, who responded with a racial slur. It then took Fox and most of the team to break up the ensuing fistfight between the two boys.

With the assistance of Dr. Charles Tucker, a young black psychologist in the Lansing school district and a former college and professional basketball player, Johnson tried to put the incident behind him. "Tuck" had met Johnson while giving a lecture at Dwight Rich Junior High School; intrigued by the youth's obvious talent and warm, open personality, the psychologist had become a friend, confidant, and mentor. He had immediately won Johnson's respect and attention by beating him in a game of one-on-one at the Dwight Rich gym in front of a crowd of the youth's friends and supporters.

Tucker's best basketball was behind him, but he was able to defeat the young phenom by strategically using some of the wiles—a well-placed elbow, a strong but not flagrant hand check, a subtle push or hold—that he had learned in the pros. Such tactics are technically illegal and often draw foul calls on the amateur level. But in the professional game, where a much more physical style of play prevails, they are commonplace and usually overlooked by the officials.

Tucker had counseled Johnson ever since their one-on-one contest on what he would have to do to excel not just at the level where he was playing but at the level that he aspired to: the NBA. Part of the process, the former pro tried to impress upon his young charge, was handling the different types of adversity he would encounter along the way. That meant learning how to deal with Fox, who had chastised Johnson for screaming at his teammate (the coach had also lambasted the other boy for not passing the ball), and finding a more productive way to deal with selfish but less talented teammates.

Stung by the racial insult, Johnson wanted to quit the team. "You're the best player out there, right?" Tucker told him. "You know it, I know it, the coach knows it, all the other players know it, now don't you think he [the ball-hogging senior] knows it too? . . . Damn right, he knows it and he doesn't like it. I wouldn't like it, either, if some young dude stepped in and took over my team. So he's frustrated, and he expressed his frustration. That's all it was. It had nothing to do with the color of your skin. Now, if you're as good as everybody thinks you are, you'll

forget the whole thing and show up tomorrow like nothing happened."

Johnson returned to the team. Yet some of the resentments and divisions lingered through the early part of the season. Though Everett was winning its games, the team had failed to come together and was not playing especially well.

It took some time for Johnson to hit his stride, too. Nervousness about living up to his reputation caused him to play poorly in the season opener, and many in attendance dismissed the buildup as hype. His play improved dramatically with each game, however, and his unselfish passing soon won him his teammates' approval. The Vikings were winning as well, and that bred contentment. With the players beginning to like and trust one another, Fox decided to ease up on some of his disciplinarian measures. He even let the teenagers listen to music in the locker

Everett High School basketball coach George Fox (top row, far left) guided the 1976-77 Vikings to a 27-1 record and the state title with a huge assist from team MVP Johnson (top row, fourth from right). Magic averaged 28.8 points and 16.8 rebounds a game and was named All-Metro, All-State, and All-American.

room before games, previously a time he had insisted be reserved for silent, solemn contemplation of the coming contest.

By midseason, Everett was undefeated and was being cited as a potential winner of the state championship tournament that was held annually at the close of the regular season. In a win over traditional rival Jackson Parkside, Johnson put on such an awesome performance—"I felt I could fly," he said—with 36 points, 18 rebounds, and 16 assists, that one sportswriter, Fred Stabley of the Lansing *State Journal*, felt a mere description of the ballplayer's exploits to be inadequate. He asked Johnson if it was all right to give him a nickname in an article about the game.

It was fine with him, Johnson replied, while thinking to himself, "Just so long as it isn't June Bug or Junior."

How about Magic? the writer asked.

The nickname was fine with the young player. There had been an earlier Magic in the basketball world: the sobriquet had been one of several carried by Earl Monroe, a Philadelphia schoolyard great turned college scoring champion and all-star professional guard whose game Johnson had studied with his father during their television sessions. The whirling, spindly Monroe was one of the most distinctive stylists the game had ever known. Johnson had even appropriated Monroe's patented spin move for his own game, and he was proud of the implied connection between his own talents and the future Hall of Famer known also as the Pearl and Black Jesus.

And so a legend was born. Articles celebrating the latest achievements of Magic Johnson and his Everett High teammates were soon appearing regularly in the sports sections of the Lansing newspapers and even in out-of-town journals. The high school sophomore had become a local celebrity.

Johnson's play may have cast a spell over all who beheld it, but there was nothing mysterious about their youngest son's success to Earvin and Christine Johnson, and they attempted constantly to reinforce the values they had instilled in him. The Vikings played their games on Friday nights. Each Saturday morning, at about six o'clock, Earvin, Sr., woke his namesake.

"How did you do last night?" he would ask the sleepy, grumbling teenager.

"We won by 20," came the typical mumbled response.

"Good," came the reply, along with a rough but affectionate shake. "Now get up; we've got work on the truck to do. You may be Magic in the gym, but you're still Junior around here." ❧

SHOOT-AROUND

AFTER MAGIC JOHNSON'S epic performance in the Jackson Parkside game, Everett High School stormed through the remainder of the 1974–75 regular season, losing only one game, to Detroit Northeastern. Expectations were high for the state tournament, but the Vikings went down in the quarterfinals to Fordson, a school in the city of Dearborn. Johnson was crushed by the loss and wept for hours afterward. "Losing shorts out my emotional circuitry," he later told Richard Levin, the cowriter of Johnson's *Magic* autobiography.

It was the way that Everett lost as much as the defeat itself that left Johnson so upset. The Vikings had led by 13 points going into the fourth quarter but had turned tentative and missed five crucial free throws in the final minutes. Two of those misses had been by Johnson, which in his own mind greatly outweighed his overall strong play.

Still, it had been a successful season, the best in a long time at Everett High. The quarterfinal loss

Johnson's spirited play made him, he said, "an instant hit" from the moment he stepped on the court as a Michigan State University freshman. "When a guy pays $3 or $4 for a ticket, I want him to get a show from me. And he will because I always have to please myself, and I always manage to do that."

galled Johnson, but it was soon overshadowed by new events in his life, new games, new challenges. He had become comfortable at Everett, and with the season over, he had time to take part in other student activities. His favorite among the several clubs and organizations he joined was *The Viking*, the school newspaper, where he served first as a reporter and then as director of advertising.

The end of the basketball season also meant more time available for working with his father on the truck or, depending on the season, shoveling snow and mowing lawns in the neighborhood or stacking boxes at his part-time job at a local dairy. "Any garages that used oil," Johnson recalled in *Magic's Touch*, "we'd come in while the shop was closed, soap down the floor, let it dry, then come back later and wash it down. Sometimes, Dad would go in and scrub the concrete floors after his shift at 2 A.M., then come home and get a few hours sleep, wake up to finish the hauling jobs, then go back to work at the plant while the rest of us were sitting down to dinner. He did that every single day. He *worked*."

There was little thought of challenging the Big E's authority. "You didn't even think about it," Earvin, Jr., recalled. "My dad didn't stand for that. He'd punish you, and he didn't care how."

Whatever resentment Junior might have felt about this schedule was outweighed by his appreciation for how hard his father worked and his recognition of how his own work ethic was beginning to pay off. "How could I refuse when *he* was working so hard?" Magic responded years later on being asked whether he ever rebelled against his father's regimen. Instead, he sought to incorporate his father's attitude into his approach to basketball.

More than a decade later, after achieving stardom in the NBA, Johnson gave a large share of the credit for his success to the Big E. "All those things paid off for me because I can see it all so clearly now," he told Roy S. Johnson, the coauthor of *Magic's Touch*. "I see everything he was trying to teach me. I look for nothing from nobody. Whatever I want, I work for. . . . He taught me about hard work. How important to me was it that he got up and worked *two* jobs every day? Very important because that was the motivation I used from the time I started playing basketball. He taught me that I wasn't going to get anything in basketball or life without working for it. That's why I get so mad when people say I'm just a flamboyant player, a guy who doesn't work hard."

To the dismay of Lansing high school coaches other than George Fox, Johnson was an even better player as a junior than he had been as a sophomore. He was now, at age 16, 6 feet 6—an inch taller than he had been the previous year—and he had added 10 pounds of muscle to his lean frame. The resentful upperclassmen who had undermined the team's unity early in the previous year had graduated, and the Vikings were now a much closer group. The team was led by Johnson and his running mate on and off the court, 5-foot 3-inch Reggie Chastine. Also, Fox was more comfortable with his star player and vice versa.

The Vikings were ranked in the top 10 in the state in the preseason polls, and they largely lived up to the great expectations. But for Johnson the season was ultimately a disappointment, for he had begun to judge himself and his teams by the most demanding of standards: anything less than a championship was unsatisfactory. Everett again lost just one regular-season game, and Johnson's play was outstanding enough for him to be named a first-team all-state selection. (He had made the second team the previous year.)

In 1976, however, the Vikings made it only to the semifinals of the state tournament before being knocked off. Their conqueror this time was Catholic Central of Detroit, and Johnson again blamed himself for the loss. He believed that as the Vikings' early lead eroded in the second half, he had been too content to pass off to his teammates rather than accept the responsibility of scoring baskets.

This self-proclaimed failure of leadership taught Johnson a valuable lesson: it is possible to be too unselfish as a player. In the closing moments of a tight game, many players suddenly display a veneer of selflessness as a means of avoiding the responsibility of taking—and perhaps missing—a crucial shot, a failure of nerve players refer to as "disappearing." Johnson had learned that there was a time in each game when it was best for the ballclub that he make a conscious effort to get each of his teammates involved in the offense by passing them the basketball, and there was a time when it was best for the team that he worry less about passing the ball and more about scoring.

Johnson was once again crushed by the defeat, but he experienced a much greater loss that summer, when Reggie Chastine was killed in an automobile accident. The news that his wisecracking, self-confident best friend had been killed devastated Magic; he ran the streets for hours that day, hoping to outdistance the pain he felt. Every so often he would sit down on the sidewalk, hang his head in his hands, and sob. Though the death made the outcome of any individual basketball contest, such as the loss to Catholic Central, seem insignificant, it only reinforced Johnson's passion for the game itself. Life was short, it seemed; better to fill it doing the things he loved.

Going into Johnson's last season at Everett, the expectations for the Vikings' prospects were exceeded only by Magic's confidence. At his suggestion, his teammates dedicated the season to the memory of

Reggie Chastine, and they crushed most of their early-season opponents. Perhaps as a reaction to his disappearing act in the state tournament the previous season, Johnson looked for his own shot as never before. He regularly threw in 30 and even 40 points a game—an outstanding total in a professional contest, which lasts 48 minutes, but even more impressive in a 32-minute high school game. On one memorable occasion, he tallied a career-high 54. He felt, he said, as if he could do anything he wanted to on the court.

Though all seemed to be going extremely well, Coach Fox foresaw problems. Magic's dominance was overwhelming even his own teammates, who had begun to feel as if they were being given little opportunity to contribute. As Johnson recounted in *Magic*, the coach called him into his office one day for a little chat.

"Earvin," Fox said, "I don't know if this is going to make any sense to you or not, but you're doing too much. You're so dominating and so good, you intimidate your teammates. They wind up standing around and watching you like everybody else in the building, including yours truly. They're reluctant to do anything for fear of making a mistake and making you mad. Our goal is to win the state championship. I know you want that more than anything in the world. So do I. But I don't know if we can do it the way you're playing now. Somewhere down the line we're going to need one of your teammates in a crucial situation and he won't be able to produce. I think if you cut your scoring to twenty-something a game we'll win it all."

To his credit, Johnson saw the wisdom in what the coach was saying, and he relinquished some of his own scoring opportunities. By midseason, Everett was undefeated. But so was its crosstown rival, Eastern High. Everett was ranked number one in the

"I became more focused," Johnson said in recalling the death of Reggie Chastine (above), Magic's high school basketball teammate and best friend who was killed in a car crash before the start of their senior year. "[Reggie] basically got myself together for me, in basketball and in life."

state; Eastern, led by Jay Vincent, the only player who could legitimately challenge Johnson's claim to basketball superiority in Lansing, was ranked number two.

Johnson and Vincent had been competing against each other, on playgrounds and in gymnasiums, since they were in grade school. Magic's team usually won, but the rivalry remained fierce and friendly. Their high school clashes were the highlight of the Lansing basketball season. Eastern had even built a new 5,000-seat gymnasium to accommodate the overflow crowds that turned out to see Eastern and Everett play one another. Nevertheless, the new arena was too small to hold all the people who wanted to see the 1977 clash between the top two teams in the state, and the game had to be moved to the fieldhouse on the Michigan State University campus.

In front of more than 10,000 fans, Eastern took an early lead and held on for the win, which vaulted the school to the top spot in the state polls. The next week, however, the team was upset by a lesser squad. Meanwhile, Everett did not lose again during the regular season.

The two powerhouses clashed once more in the first round of the state tournament. The game was held in the Eastern gym but televised live throughout the area. This time, Johnson led Everett to an easy win, while Vincent was held to a single basket. Confident and focused, the Vikings rolled over the rest of the competition in the tournament, until the finals. Then a gritty squad from Brother Rice High School in Birmingham put up an extremely tough fight before succumbing in overtime.

Everett was the state champ, but Magic had only a short time to enjoy the satisfaction of his team's accomplishment. Shortly after the tournament was over, he traveled to West Germany with a group of high school all-stars. And as soon as he returned to

Lansing, he found himself under intense pressure to decide which university he would attend in the fall.

College basketball in the United States is an extremely big business, and Johnson had been besieged by recruiters from literally hundreds of colleges since he was a sophomore in high school. Each day, dozens of recruitment letters filled his family's mailbox. Finally, Dr. Frank Throop, the Everett principal, volunteered to have one of his secretaries handle this correspondence.

Meanwhile, articles speculating about which college had the edge in the contest to gain Magic's services appeared daily in the Lansing newspapers. Recruiters called and even visited the Johnson home at all hours and waylaid Magic in the hallways at school between classes. All of them offered full athletic scholarships, but many offered illegal inducements as well: cars, prostitutes, under-the-table payments to Magic, coaching jobs for Dr. Charles Tucker and Coach Fox, a cushy job for the Big E. The process quickly grew wearisome for the high school senior. There were too many "phony smiles, insincere speeches, and illegal offers," he said.

Johnson was frank about what he wanted in a university: a solid basketball program through which he would have a good chance to win a national championship and a coach who believed in the running game. Though he was a solid student with a 2.8 average, a university education was a secondary consideration. He acknowledged its importance; his father constantly said to him, "I don't want you to end up in this factory like I did." But Magic regarded a college degree more as a safety net, should he suffer a debilitating injury or should his pro career not pan out, rather than a primary concern.

With considerable input from his father and Tuck, Johnson decided to attend Michigan State, which was located in East Lansing, just a few miles

Johnson glides into the air to toss his trademark no-look pass during a February 1978 contest between Michigan State Unviersity and the University of Illinois. Magic learned at an early age, "If I'm going to throw a no-look pass, I want to be sure somebody's going to catch it."

from his home. The choice was something of a surprise in that the Spartans did not have a history of basketball success. Michigan State had not won the championship of its league, the Big Ten, or qualified for the National Collegiate Athletic Association (NCAA) tournament, which determines the national collegiate champion, since 1959. And the Spartans' new coach, Jud Heathcote, had a reputation for screaming at and berating his players to motivate them, a coaching style that Johnson disdained.

But Michigan State was close to home, and it had a nucleus of promising players, such as the quick-jumping forward Greg Kelser and Magic's old rival and friend Jay Vincent. Johnson had grown fascinated with the prospect of leading the perennial hoops also-rans to national basketball prominence. "If you think you're that good, then you make the program," Tuck told him. "Don't worry about going to a school that already has one."

At Michigan State, Johnson was an immediate success on and off the court. His warm personality and ready smile won him friends immediately, as they seemed to do everywhere he went. He roomed in the dorms with Vincent, earned a B average in his first semester (his major was telecommunications), and spun records at a popular nightspot near the campus, where he was known as E. J. the Deejay. His fellow students treated him like a celebrity before he ever laced up a pair of sneakers for Michigan State.

Johnson's popularity increased once he stepped on the court. Even though his overanxiousness and nervousness contributed to an unimpressive college debut—"I kept waiting for you do something . . . waiting and waiting and waiting," a disappointed friend told him afterward—Johnson soon put his jitters behind him and began to excel. Michigan State promptly raced out to an insurmountable lead in the Big Ten.

At 6 feet 8, Vincent, the team's center, was the same height as Johnson, the point guard, and Kelser, the leading scorer and rebounder, and so the under-sized Spartans relied on quickness rather than brawn. They frequently overwhelmed their opponents with the fast break, which often culminated spectacularly with Magic throwing a pinpoint lob above the rim that the soaring Kelser corraled and slammed through the hoop on his way down.

In the regional final of the NCAA tournament, the Spartans suffered a disappointing loss to the eventual champions, the University of Kentucky Wildcats. Heathcote, trying to nurse a small lead, mistakenly ordered his fleetfooted players to slow the pace and thus allowed their much bigger but pon-derous opponents to rally. Nevertheless, the 1977–78 basketball season was Michigan State's most success-ful ever, and Magic reaped most of the accolades.

A unanimous selection for the All-Big Ten Team, Johnson had averaged 17 points, 8 rebounds, and 7 assists per game. But statistics were an inadequate measure of his overall contribution to the Spartans' sterling 25-5 record. Heathcote tried to explain: "In Earvin's case you don't talk about the points he scores. Rather, it's the points he produces. And that doesn't mean just the baskets and assists, but the first pass that makes the second pass possible. He's con-scious of scoring himself, but it isn't an obsession with him."

Johnson reiterated that his emphasis was on get-ting baskets for his team, not for himself. "My whole game is court sense," he said. "Being smart, taking charge, setting up a play, or, if I have to, scoring."

The greatest compliment to Johnson's abilities came during the spring of 1978, following the conclusion of the Michigan State season. That year, the team with the first pick in the NBA draft was the Kansas City Kings, and they wanted to use it to select Johnson. The 18-year-old college freshman, said Kings general manager Joe Axelson, "could start for anybody in the league right now. He's the most exciting college player I've ever seen. I can't believe God created a six-foot-eight-inch player who can handle the ball like that." ❦

5

THAT CHAMPIONSHIP
SEASON

❦

MAGIC JOHNSON WAS flattered and genuinely intrigued by the Kansas City Kings' interest in him. The temptation to immediately realize his dream of playing in the NBA was great, as was the lure of the big money the Kings were offering. And by entering the league at age 18, he would make history as the youngest player ever to be selected first in the NBA draft.

But Johnson opted to stay in school in 1978. He was having fun at Michigan State, both on and off the court, and his father and Charles Tucker impressed upon him that his game would benefit from a little more seasoning. The determining factor, however, was Johnson's belief that Michigan State, with its three best players returning to school that fall, had a legitimate chance of winning the NCAA title.

The pundits agreed. Michigan State was ranked number seven nationally in the preseason polls. *Sports Illustrated* even went so far as to put Johnson on the front of its annual college basketball preview issue. For the first of the many times he would grace the magazine's cover, he wore a tuxedo, a top hat, patent leather shoes, and his trademark huge smile while soaring above the rim to tip in a basketball.

Playing in front of capacity crowds at home and on the road, the Michigan State Spartans won 10 of

Johnson slams the ball through the hoop during Michigan State's showdown against Indiana State University for the 1979 National Collegiate Athletic Association (NCAA) championship. The only freshman in the country to make the All–Big Ten Team and All-American in 1978, Magic proved to be an even greater force on the court as a sophomore, when he was honored as the NCAA tournament's most valuable player.

69

their first 11 games; the team's only loss was to perennial national powerhouse North Carolina, and then only by a single point. Yet the early-season success masked some serious problems with Jud Heathcote's squad. The unprecedented expectations for the team mounted with each victory and created unprecedented pressure to succeed. Heathcote was among those who did not respond well. He seemed to get tighter and more sharp-tongued with each win, and his nervousness rubbed off on his players.

Soon the Spartans were playing not to lose rather than to win. As had happened in the NCAA tournament contest against Kentucky the previous year, Heathcote was ordering his charges to play a slow-down, protective style rather than the running, attacking game for which the team was best suited. Sometimes, it seemed, he had his players protecting a lead before they even had one.

The ballplayers, Johnson foremost among them, were growing increasingly frustrated. They knew they were best when they were free to react and run, which gave them an opportunity to use their advantage in quickness to offset their relative lack of size. Though he respected Heathcote's passion for winning, Magic was growing tired of the coach's shouting, particularly once he stopped allowing the players to express their own ideas in practice. Although exceedingly receptive to coaching, Johnson was used to verbalizing his own ideas about tactics and strategy in practice sessions. Heathcote had begun to cut him off, especially anytime his star point guard broached the idea of Michigan State's quickening the tempo.

By the midpoint in the regular season, the divisions were beginning to show. The Spartans lost four of six contests to Big Ten rivals, including an ignominious 18-point thrashing by league doormat Northwestern that left Michigan State four games behind the conference leader, Ohio State. For the first time all year, the Spartans found themselves out of the top 20 in the two major basketball polls.

To Heathcote's credit, he reconsidered his approach in the wake of the losses. In the days before an important contest with Ohio State, he held a team meeting in which each player was encouraged to speak out about what had gone wrong with the team and how it could be fixed. Together, the players and coaches decided that from that point onward they would run the fast break at every opportunity. The ball would be in Magic's hands; it would be up to him to push it upcourt for the full 40 minutes.

With Vincent scoring from the low post, Kelser running the floor and soaring for lob passes, and Johnson pounding the ball down the middle of the floor, shoulders low, his dribble high, eyes darting from side to side in search of a cutting teammate, Michigan State ran Ohio State and their next eight opponents right off the floor. Though the Spartans dropped their final regular-season game, to Wisconsin, the loss was not especially meaningful. The winning streak had given the Spartans a share of their second-straight Big Ten title and, more important, their second straight invitation to the NCAA tournament.

Having changed his tactics to take better advantage of his best player's skills, Heathcote was eager to sing Johnson's praises. "He's the best player in the open court today," the coach proclaimed. "If Earvin stays in college all four years, he'll be remembered as the player who put the pass back into the game. Bob Cousy [the great Boston Celtics guard of the 1950s, renowned for his ball-handling skill] showed people the value of the pass on the fast break. Earvin is showing what it can do for an entire offense. And that's because his court vision is so tremendous."

Michigan State's outstanding play carried on right into the NCAA tournament. The team rolled

The tandem of Johnson (left) and All-American forward Greg Kelser (right), the chief recipient of Magic's pinpoint passing at Michigan State and the team's leading scorer, spearheaded the Spartan's run for the 1979 national championship. "A little eye contact is all we need," said Kelser, who scored many of his points on lob passes from Johnson. "I know what [Magic's] looking for, and he knows what I'm looking for."

over its first three opponents—Lamar, Louisiana State, and Notre Dame—by an average of 20 points, despite losing the services of Vincent. He suffered a stress fracture of his right foot in the first game.

The most satisfying victory, for many reasons, was the win over Notre Dame. Like many players, Johnson and his teammates felt that year in and year out the Notre Dame squad, and especially its egotistical coach, Richard ("Digger") Phelps—the epitome of the self-aggrandizing college coach who exalted himself at the expense of his players—received much more attention and favorable publicity than was warranted by their basketball accomplishments. "We wanted Digger Phelps so badly we could taste it," Johnson said of himself and his teammates. "When you play Notre Dame, you play Digger. As head coach, he makes sure he's the whole show."

Many analysts expected the extremely deep and talented Notre Dame team to win easily. "Notre Dame goes at you with nine players, and we come back at you with two," said Heathcote, referring to Johnson and Kelser; after Vincent was injured, they were the only Spartans who were regarded as being especially talented. And Phelps believed he had a weapon to negate Johnson in the person of 6-foot-7-inch guard Bill Hanzlik, who was rightly regarded as a superb defensive player.

Kelser, among other Spartans, laughed derisively when asked to comment on Hanzlik's chances to stop Johnson. "If it were me," the acrobatic, high-scoring Spartan forward said, "I'd say something about his mother and then hope he'd hit me and get thrown out of the game."

As it turned out, an ejection was the only chance the Fighting Irish had of stopping Magic and the Spartans. The game's pattern was established at the opening tip-off, when Kelser outleaped the much taller Notre Dame center and tapped the ball to Johnson in the frontcourt. The Spartan guard gathered it in and without even turning his head flung a perfect pass over his shoulder to a streaking Mike Brkovich, who soared for the jam. Notre Dame remained a step behind all game, and Michigan State won easily. Kelser scored 34 points; however, Johnson, who tallied 13 assists and, as ever, led the fast break, was the key. "That's our offense," said his backcourt mate, Terry Donnelly. "One passes and the other one dunks."

Donnelly was more expansive about what Johnson's personality and skills meant to the Spartans: Magic, he said, had "a personality that's like Muhammad Ali's. It's classy, not conceited or anything. There have been times when he was actually running down the floor telling jokes. He's always smiling, always laughing. Never a frown on his face. Everybody likes a guy like that. . . . I had heard the stories even before Magic arrived on campus. But it didn't really hit me until I got in the backcourt with him the first day of practice. You're running down the floor and you're open. Most people can't get the ball to you through two or three people, but with Magic all of a sudden the ball is in your hands and you've got a lay-up."

The win over Notre Dame propelled Michigan State to the national semifinals—the so-called Final Four—of the NCAA tournament, which in 1979 were held in Salt Lake City, Utah. The Spartans' opponent was the University of Pennsylvania, a rather lightly regarded team from the athletically weak Ivy League that had scored a series of upsets over seemingly more talented teams. Penn's Cinderella run came to an end against Michigan State, which dominated play from the outset and posted humiliating leads of 38–8 and then 50–17 at halftime.

The game that changed the course of basketball: Johnson (left) and Larry Bird (center) face each other for the first time as Michigan State battles Indiana State for the national championship on March 26, 1979. With Jay Vincent (right) and the rest of Magic's teammates dogging Bird all over the court, the Sycamores fell to the Spartans, 75–64.

The final was 101–67 in favor of the Spartans, with Magic totaling 29 points, 10 assists, and 10 rebounds.

The Michigan State rout made possible the matchup the basketball world had been awaiting since virtually the start of the season, for the winner of the other semifinal contest had been Indiana State. Undefeated and ranked number one in the nation, the Sycamores were led by a 6-foot 10-inch blond-haired forward named Larry Joe Bird, whose marvelous performance—35 points, 16 rebounds, and 9 assists—in his team's semifinal victory over powerful De Paul was all the more impressive in that he played with a triple fracture of his left thumb. Like Magic, with whom he has become forever linked in the memory of appreciative basketball fans, Bird had led a university team that was a perennial hoops doormat to national roundball prominence.

By the time Michigan State met Indiana State, Johnson and Bird were by far the best-known and most popular college players in the country. Their appeal was based on similar elements in their game. They both could score baskets, especially Bird, who averaged more than 30 points a game during the three years he played for Indiana State. But it was the way the two players passed that truly captured the fans' imagination. Both ballplayers possessed an uncanny ability to spot the open man and get him the basketball, often in a most spectacular fashion.

Like Johnson, the Indiana State star had honed his skills by spending countless hours on outdoor courts, in Bird's case near his homes in the small towns of West Baden and French Lick, Indiana. Even in a state where basketball is something of a secular religion, Bird's persistence stood out. The sight of the tall, skinny youngster shooting by himself in long solitary sessions—sometimes until deep into the night, when only the echoing thump of the basketball alerted passersby to the boy's presence—had become common in "the valley," as its denizens referred to the impoverished region where Bird was born and raised.

The court was the one place where the gangly boy seemed for a time to be able to escape from the chaos of a home life dominated by violence, the grimmest (even by the standards of the valley) poverty, and the problems of an alcoholic father who would ultimately kill himself. Off the court, there was little about his life that young Larry Bird could control; but on the court he could rely on himself. Over time, as he developed his talent, his successes on the basketball

Johnson waves to the more than 10,000 Michigan State basketball fans who packed Jenison Fieldhouse to pay tribute to the Spartans on March 27, one day after the team captured the 1979 NCAA championship. "We had a mission to accomplish," Magic told the crowd, "and we did it!"

court provided the withdrawn youngster with a self-esteem that enabled him to overcome the stigma of his upbringing. It was, despite the whiteness of Bird's skin, an unbringing that in many ways was more typical of most of the black players he would join in the professional ranks than Johnson's was.

By the spring of 1979, Bird had already endured a marriage and divorce in addition to his troubled childhood and his father's suicide, and the 22-year-old's difficult past had left him a less immediately charismatic public figure than Michigan State's star player. Whereas Bird was tight-lipped, remote, and wary of reporters and attention, Johnson was outgoing, upbeat, and seemed to welcome and thrive on the media's interest in him. The contrast in personalities only seemed to add spice to the heavily anticipated matchup between their respective teams.

The arena in Salt Lake City would have been sold out no matter which two teams wound up vying for the collegiate championship. But the number of television viewers who tuned in to watch Michigan State and Indiana State play was the truest demonstration of Bird's and Magic's appeal. The contest drew the largest audience for a basketball game in the history of televised sports.

As is often true of such heavily anticipated and publicized events, the game itself was something of an anticlimax. But from Johnson's point of view it represented the fulfillment of a dream. If Michigan State had, as Heathcote had joked, only two real players, then Indiana State boasted only one. The Spartans double-teamed Bird from the outset, making it very difficult for his teammates to get him the ball. Meanwhile, the Sycamores proved unable to contend with the duo of Johnson and Kelser. Michigan State led by 9 points at halftime and by 16 in the second half; a late Indiana State rally fell short, and when the final buzzer sounded, Bird was on the bench sobbing, his face buried in a towel, and the Spartans were on top by 11.

Johnson scored 24 points and grabbed 8 rebounds, and Kelser scored 19 and nabbed 7 boards. Bird had scored 19 points and garnered 13 rebounds, but hampered by his broken thumb, he had shot poorly. Indiana State's loss was its only one in 34 games that year, and Bird was honored as the college basketball player of the year. But Magic and Michigan State had taken the big prize: the national championship. ❧

6

THE MAGIC TOUCH

❦

According to Jerry West, the former Los Angeles Lakers star and the general manager who made Johnson the number one pick in the 1979 NBA draft, "Different players can teach you different things about the game of basketball. Some can teach you how to shoot with the proper form; others are skillful passers, rebounders, or defensive geniuses. Magic Johnson epitomizes all those skills in one package better than anyone who has ever played the game."

No SOONER HAD the 1979 national champion Michigan State Spartans been honored with a tumultuous rally on campus than Magic Johnson began to be besieged with *the* question: Would he return for another year of college ball, or would he turn pro? There were more factors to consider in making his decision this time around. He had attained his goal of winning a national title, and both his father and Charles Tucker felt there was little more he could learn by playing in the college ranks.

Because Boston Celtics mastermind Arnold ("Red") Auerbach, in the kind of keen maneuver that had made his reputation, had secured the playing rights to Larry Bird a year earlier, Johnson was virtually assured again of being the first player selected in the NBA draft. But this time the team that chose him would be, through a combination of circumstances, not one of the league's worst but one of its best. The Los Angeles Lakers owned the top pick by virtue of a trade several years earlier, in which they fobbed off aging but high-scoring guard Gail Goodrich to the undermanned New Orleans Jazz in exchange for the Jazz's first pick in the 1979 draft. New Orleans needed much more help than Goodrich could provide, and to the club's chagrin it was now time to pay the price for its shortsighted decision.

The prospect of joining the Lakers and their star players Kareem Abdul-Jabbar, the exceedingly smooth forward Jamaal ("Silk") Wilkes, and quick guard Norm Nixon appealed to Johnson much more than the thought of joining the hapless Kansas City Kings. In college, a single dominant player can, as Magic had shown at Michigan State and Bird at Indiana State, make a team a winner. But that rarely happens in the professional ranks.

If Johnson stayed at Michigan State, the likelihood was that he would be drafted by a very weak team when he decided to turn pro. If he wanted to play for a winner immediately, entering the draft in 1979 was his best chance. In addition, Los Angeles was a large, sophisticated city in which he was likely to receive a lot of media attention as well as the opportunity for commercial endorsements and other means of supplementing his income.

All these factors made the decision an easy one for Johnson. At a press conference held by the Lakers in Los Angeles in May 1979, Chick Hearn, the team's longtime announcer, introduced the Michigan State star to the media by saying that he could not remember "a young man in years, maybe ever, who has captivated fans the way Magic has." The contract that Johnson and his advisers eventually negotiated with Los Angeles made him, at $500,000 per year, very briefly—that is, until Bird signed his contract with the Celtics—the highest-paid rookie in NBA history.

The Lakers had immediate cause to consider the money well spent. Training camp began in October, and though Johnson professed to be somewhat surprised by the size and sophistication of the city of Los Angeles and at how physical the pro game was, few adjustment problems were evident. His Laker teammates immediately and respectfully noted how hard he practiced—with an intensity that led to a few

Christine and Earvin Johnson, Sr., are a couple of proud parents after learning that their son Earvin, Jr., was the first player chosen in the 1979 NBA draft. Being the number one draft choice helped him become the highest-paid rookie in league history.

verbal skirmishes and even some fisticuffs—and hung a new nickname on him, Buck, for "young buck," a reference to Johnson's tirelessness. (Throughout his career with Los Angeles, he would usually be referred to by teammates and coaches as Buck or Earvin, rarely Magic.)

As always, Johnson's talent was a revelation. Jerry West, the former Laker great who had become the team's general manager, had believed that Magic, with his size and strength, would be a power forward in the pros. But when the longtime backcourt star saw the youngster's ball-handling skills every day in practice it became obvious that Johnson had to play guard.

Equally exciting to those who watched Johnson every day was his enthusiasm for the game. The long NBA season—82 games in the regular season, plus 15 to 25 more in the playoffs for a good team, compared to a maximum of 35 games in college ball—is an enervating succession of one-night stands played out across the country. The games themselves are exceptionally demanding from a physical standpoint—much more so than baseball, for example, which is the only major American professional sport that plays as many—and the schedule is also draining mentally and emotionally.

For a number of NBA franchises, a good portion of the regular-season games are, to a certain extent, meaningless. With two-thirds of the teams qualifying each year for the playoffs (the so-called real, or second, season), a single contest might be viewed as not very crucial by its participants, particularly when one of the teams has just played five games in eight nights in five different cities thousands of miles apart. The perception held by many basketball fans, rightly or wrongly, was that most NBA players essentially paced themselves and coasted through the regular season, reserving their best efforts for particularly important games—especially, said cynics, those that were televised nationally—and the playoffs.

Such perceptions were part of an even larger public relations problem that existed for the NBA at the time that Johnson entered the league. In the previous year, 12 of the league's 22 teams had reported dramatic drops in attendance, including the teams in four of the league's biggest markets: Chicago, Los Angeles, New York, and Philadelphia. National television ratings were down 26 percent, and for the upcoming year the networks did not even plan to carry live several of the games in the championship series—an unprecedented condemnation of the league's drawing power.

The falloff in interest was the result of several factors. Over the past decade, many of the league's greatest stars—including Elgin Baylor, Wilt Chamberlain, Walt Frazier, John Havlicek, Earl Monroe, Oscar Robertson, Bill Russell, Jerry West—had retired. But with the exception of the flamboyant Julius Erving and the often-injured Bill Walton, equally exciting new talent had yet to emerge.

To make matters worse, drug scandals and polls contributed to the belief that a majority of NBA players used drugs of some kind. At the same time, the public perceived a sense of indifference among most ballplayers and stereotyped them as being more interested in scoring statistics than in winning ballgames. NBA players, it was felt, were apt to put forth a subpar effort on any given night.

According to some analysts, the crux of the NBA's problem was the huge number of blacks in the league. The vast majority of American society, including the audience for professional sports, was white, yet 75 percent of the players were black. Some people charged that whites were unwilling to patronize a sport so dominated by blacks.

In the end, most of the negative stereotypes held about NBA players were focused on the league's black members. The success of the relatively few white stars was much more apt to be attributed to grit, hustle, determination, hard work, and intelligence than was the achievement of the NBA's numerous black superstars, who were credited with "natural talent." These critics of the pro game claimed that blacks were undisciplined, more prone to one-on-one play, and generally in more need of coaching than their white counterparts.

Paul Silas, a longtime NBA player and coach, spelled out part of the problem. Basketball players had become so good they made the game look easy, and they received extremely high salaries to boot. "People in general do not look favorably upon blacks who are making large sums of money," Silas said, "if it appears they are not working hard for that money."

Though the audience for basketball remained large, an ever-greater share was being claimed by the college game. Many people said the enthusiasm of the players was much more evident at the college level, where, it so happened, more white players held prominent roles. In addition, the alleged penchant of blacks for undisciplined play was kept in check by

The Los Angeles Lakers' rookie point guard rounds the bases while playing for the Magic Johnson Enterprises softball team at a game in Lansing. Unlike a number of NBA rookies, Johnson put most of his salary into the bank, investments, and his own business, such as Magic Johnson Enterprises.

powerful college taskmasters such as Lou Carnesecca, Bobby Knight, Dean Smith, and other prominent coaches who attempted to dictate every aspect of the game from the sideline. If the NBA was, as the truism held, preeminently a "player's league," where quickness and speed ruled and the ability of a coach to influence events on the floor was limited, then college basketball, with its slower pace, zone defenses, and absence of a shot clock, marked the height of the coach's influence.

In large part, the criticisms many people leveled at NBA basketball evoked the problems George Fox initially faced with Magic Johnson's game: they interpreted the fast-paced, undeniably flamboyant style of play as inherently undisciplined and dangerously contemptuous of the fundamentals. Just like jazz, which emphasizes improvisation in a song but was at one time condemned as "jungle music" performed by ignorant musicians innocent of the classical tradition, NBA ball in the late 1970s, which emphasized the individual creative talents of its players within a team context, was stigmatized as a "black" thing.

Pro basketball, its critics said, reflected the sport as it was supposedly played by black Americans in the inner cities rather than the allegedly purer variety played on college campuses under the watchful eyes of stern white coaches. Yet that criticism owed more to the racial makeup of the league than to the style of play. In fact, professional basketball of the 1950s—supposedly a golden era of fundamental purity—was played at a much more breakneck pace than the modern game. Back then, however, the majority of its practitioners were white.

It was in this context that the evident joy with which Johnson played basketball, coupled with his celebrated unselfishness, became so important. No one could criticize him, as they did the often aloof Kareem Abdul-Jabbar, for the coolness of his approach or for going through the motions. Nor could anyone accuse Magic of putting individual statistics ahead of winning.

Some people wondered whether Johnson's ebullient "college" approach could successfully be carried over to the pros. "You have to remember that happiness and glow and joy have a way of turning to dust in our league," said Pat Williams, general manager of the Philadelphia 76ers. But few doubted the Laker rookie's talent.

In the early weeks of the 1979–80 season, it became clear that both Johnson's attitude and skill were equally integral parts of his game. In the season opener, when Abdul-Jabbar hit a skyhook just before the final buzzer to give the Lakers a one-point victory over the San Diego Clippers, an overjoyed Magic raced across the court, leaped into the regal center's arms, and enveloped him in a bear hug. At first, Johnson's teammates seemed unsure of how to respond. Previously, the Lakers, a Los Angeles

Try as they might, Julius Erving (right), Darryl Dawkins (center), and the rest of the Philadelphia 76ers found it difficult to contain Johnson in the 1980 NBA finals. The rookie sensation piloted the Lakers to a three-games-to-two lead in the series, then switched from guard to center for Game 6 and scored 42 points while grabbing 15 rebounds to help Los Angeles clinch the championship.

sportswriter had written, "seem[ed] to win or lose with a shrug." But in an instant Abdul-Jabbar was grinning and returning the rookie's embrace in the midst of a welter of similarly jubilant and celebratory teammates.

Sportswriters and teammates were soon claiming that they detected a change in Abdul-Jabbar's approach. The 10-year NBA veteran's attitude toward the game seemed to be rejuvenated, and many people attributed the difference to Johnson's energizing effect. "It's not Kareem's way to be jumping up and down all the time," said Norm Nixon, "but you can tell he's more enthusiastic now."

The generosity of Magic's game also attracted notice. The Lakers won regularly, mixing a devastating fast break with the potency of Abdul-Jabbar in the low post, and much of the credit went to Johnson. "The first thing Magic brought here was a big helping of enthusiasm and excitement," said Jack McKinney, the team's coach. "I think it's been infectious. It also helps, too, when a new player with the kind of advance press notices he had spends most of the game trying to pass the ball to teammates."

Paul Westhead, who took over as the Lakers head coach after McKinney suffered a near-fatal head injury in a bicycling accident on November 8, 1979, said, "If you look at his nickname, 'Magic,' you would think all he does is make fancy passes. But he is as much a bread-and-butter guard as he is a passer. He'll take the ball down the lane in traffic and he'll also rebound. That's why he's so respected by his teammates. He gets down in the trenches, too, but he can still make the Bob Cousy–type pass."

Sparked by Johnson, who averaged 18 points and almost 8 assists and 8 rebounds a game, the Lakers won 60 of their 82 regular-season games—13 more than the previous season—and improved their standing in the Pacific Division from third to first. In the Atlantic Division, Larry Bird was having an even greater effect on his club. The proud Boston Celtics, who had posted just 29 victories the previous year, won 61 games in 1979–80, the greatest single-season improvement in NBA history. Bird had averaged 21 points, 10 rebounds, and nearly 5 assists per game.

Slowly but surely, Johnson's joyous involvement in his team's fortunes and Bird's grim determination had begun to effect a change in the public's attitude toward professional basketball. As the style and substance of Magic's and Bird's play each night rubbed off on their colleagues, the criticism that had plagued the NBA in the late 1970s was steadily chipped away. Though the process would take several years in all, the league would become renowned for having the brightest, most physically gifted, and hardest-working athletes in all of sports.

Bird was honored with the NBA's 1980 Rookie of the Year Award, but Johnson once again copped the biggest prize. In the playoffs, the Lakers dispatched the Phoenix Suns and the defending champion Seattle SuperSonics in just five games apiece to capture the Western Conference title. Meanwhile, Julius Erving and the Philadelphia 76ers had upset the Celtics in five games to claim the Eastern Conference crown.

Los Angeles and Philadelphia split the first two games of the 1980 NBA finals, which were played at the Los Angeles Forum, and the series stood deadlocked again after the next two games were played at the Spectrum in Philadelphia. Abdul-Jabbar led the Lakers to a 108–103 victory in Game 5, but he did not have an easy time of it. Midway through the third quarter, he severely sprained his left ankle and had to be helped to the locker room. He hobbled back onto the court for the fourth quarter, with his injured ankle heavily swathed in tape, and somehow managed to score 14 points, to give him a total of 40 for the game. But he was finished for the series.

Without their big man, who had averaged nearly 34 points and 14 rebounds a game in the previous five contests, Los Angeles now seemed to stand little chance against Philadelphia. In Erving, Darryl Dawkins, Bobby Jones, and Caldwell Jones, the Sixers boasted the tallest, strongest, and deepest front line in the game. As the Lakers boarded the plane that would take them to Philadelphia for Game 6, Westhead told his rookie point guard that he would have to fill in for the disabled Abdul-Jabbar as the team's center. In effect, the coach was also asking Johnson to assume Abdul-Jabbar's burden of being the team's leading scorer.

"That's fine with me," Magic replied. He assumed that the coach could not be serious about matching up a point guard against Dawkins, the Sixers' huge center, who stood more than 7 feet tall and weighed almost 300 pounds. On the flight east, Johnson played along with the joke, taking Abdul-Jabbar's customary seat on the plane and reassuring his teammates, "Don't worry, the Big Fella's here."

At the shoot-around the day of the game, Johnson learned that Westhead was serious when the coach had him run through some plays in the center position. The strategy was a tribute to Magic's all-around skills, and by gametime he felt confident rather than nervous about combating Philadelphia's huge forwards and centers. He even went so far as to assure reporters that there would be no seventh game because the Lakers were going to win Game 6 and claim the championship.

The Los Angeles players got together before the game and resolved that without Abdul-Jabbar, who was better suited for a half-court game, they would run even more than usual—after made baskets as well as missed shots and turnovers. And that was exactly what they did. The Lakers ran the fast break relentlessly, and Johnson used every move from his hoopsy-doopsy days on the Lansing playgrounds to bedevil the bigger, slower-footed Philadelphia defenders. By the time the final buzzer sounded, he had tallied 42 points, grabbed 15 rebounds, passed for 7 assists, and recorded 6 steals. He had put on one of the greatest performances in the history of the NBA playoffs in helping Los Angeles win the game, 123–107, and take the league title.

In light of Johnson's seasonlong contributions and his Game 6 spectacular, it can fairly be said that no rookie in history, with the exception of the hallowed Bill Russell, had ever contributed as much to an NBA championship team as had Magic Johnson, who was named the most valuable player of the playoffs. "Magic thinks every season goes like that," Westhead said in the Los Angeles locker room after the game. "You play some games, win the title, and get named MVP." ☙

7

SHOWTIME

❦

A heart-stopping sight to opposing players at the Los Angeles Forum: Johnson pushes the ball upcourt in the high-energy, high-speed Laker style of basketball known as Showtime. "All he wants to do is get the ball to somebody else and let him score," observed teammate Kareem Abdul-Jabbar. "If you're a basketball player, you've got to love somebody like that."

IT INDEED SEEMED as if Magic Johnson enjoyed a charmed basketball life, but his second season in the NBA proved to be the most challenging of his entire hoops career to date and demonstrated that even he could make no assumptions about his roundball success. In November 1980, just 20 games into the season, with the Los Angeles Lakers riding high atop the Pacific Division with a 15 and 5 record and Johnson scoring more than 20 points a game, as well as leading the league in assists and steals and the league's guards in rebounding, he tore cartilage in his left knee. He underwent immediate surgery.

The injury, said Johnson, who had never been seriously hurt before, made him "see that just as fast as you can rise to the top, you can come tumbling down. You lose the ball and you lose being around your teammates. That's what really hurts. I've always enjoyed the entire experience of basketball, being part of a team. All of a sudden that's taken away, and that's not easy."

Despite the doubts that plagued Johnson during the long, lonely weeks of recovery and rehabilitation, the injury was not genuinely career threatening. Its greatest effect was on the fortunes of the Lakers, manifesting itself, somewhat surprisingly, not while Magic was recuperating but after his return to action. Led by Kareem Abdul-Jabbar, who was scoring more points than he had in five seasons, Johnson's talented teammates banded together and won 28 of the 45 games he missed, a winning percentage not quite as high as the previous season's but excellent nonetheless and good enough for second place in the division.

When Johnson returned near the end of the regular season, it was assumed that his services would enable the Lakers to improve their play enough to win a second straight championship. The dynamics of a winning basketball team are fragile, however, and Magic's return, instead of helping, actually hurt the Lakers.

Attendance had dipped down at the Forum during Johnson's absence, and his first game back was heavily promoted as "The Magic Is Back" Night. A sellout crowd and a media horde was on hand for the game against the lowly New Jersey Nets, but some of the Lakers regarded the behavior of the fans and the sporting press as a slight to their own accomplishments and abilities and resented the fact that so much attention was being paid to an individual player rather than to the team. Johnson was being hailed as a savior; in their professional pride, his fellow Lakers did not think that they needed to be saved.

"He's just one guy," said Abdul-Jabbar, the team captain. "He's special, with great instincts and ability, but we're a team." Another Laker denounced the hype surrounding Magic's return as "a circus."

In some ways, the resentment that surfaced among the Lakers was only partly related to Johnson's injury. All of his teammates were older than he was and had much more experience in the league than he did. None of them, with the exception of Abdul-Jabbar, was as highly paid, and none received the

Detroit Pistons guard Isiah Thomas (right) and Johnson go head-to-head in the 1984 NBA All-Star Game. Except for 1981 and 1989, when injuries kept him sidelined, Magic played in the All-Star Game every year he was in the league.

kind of media attention or opportunity for lucrative commercial endorsements that Magic already did. More than one talented veteran team in NBA history had already been figuratively destroyed as a result of the money and attention paid to a high-profile newcomer.

So long as Johnson was on the court with the Lakers, contributing to the team's success and demonstrating with his remarkable and generous play the reason why he was so richly rewarded, the resentments remained hidden. Once he was injured and his teammates had to come closer together in his absence if they wished to overcome his loss, the complaints surfaced. In addition, several of the players were angry about the overall situation regarding the team, which they believed had been harmed even more by Coach Paul Westhead's increasingly dictatorial and uncommunicative style than by Magic's injury.

Johnson felt the difference both on and off the court in the way his teammates reacted to his presence. On the court, the Lakers had problems adjusting their game to accommodate his return to the floor. The team's other usual starting guard, the multitalented Norm Nixon, for example, had assumed the duties of the point guard in Johnson's absence. Nixon, after all, had been the team's primary ballhandler before Magic joined the Lakers.

When Johnson was in the lineup prior to his injury, Nixon would race downcourt to fill a lane or spot up for a jump shot in the Laker fast break. In Magic's absence, Nixon had been instructed to go to the center of the court for an outlet pass and then to bring the ball upcourt—a habit he instinctively continued after Johnson came back from his injury. Accordingly, the two guards often found themselves racing to occupy the same spot on the court to receive an outlet pass or to start a play. Sometimes, embarassingly, Johnson and Nixon even collided as they ran for the same position.

Off the court, for the first time in his career, Johnson felt like an outsider among his teammates, excluded from their conversations and horseplay. The camaraderie that had helped fuel the team's championship drive the previous season seemed to be long gone. Though the Lakers won 11 of the 17 regular-season games that remained on their schedule when Magic returned, they were not especially impressive in doing so, and the players sensed that the right chemistry was not there.

The situation worsened just before the start of Los Angeles's three-game opening-round playoff series with the Houston Rockets. Nixon was quoted in a newspaper article as saying that Johnson's desire to handle the ball took away from his—Nixon's—game. Johnson's backcourt mate went on to say that Magic hogged publicity and endorsements as well as the ball. Johnson's response—"Now everybody spends more time worrying about getting his share and worrying about what the other guy is getting than winning games"—only added to the disagreement.

Amid this atmosphere of dissension and recriminations—the Lakers could still be seen arguing as they took the court for Game 3—Los Angeles dropped the series to Houston. In the third and deciding game, with the Lakers down to their last possession and trailing by a point, Westhead diagrammed a play designed to get the ball to Abdul-Jabbar for the final shot. Johnson was supposed to make the pass to the Lakers center, but Houston double-teamed Abdul-Jabbar. Magic had a split second in which to make a decision; he determined to drive the middle instead of passing the ball.

Challenged in the lane, Johnson threw up an awkward leaning shot that touched nothing—an embarrassing "airball" that brought a humiliating end to the Lakers' reign as champions. It was the lowest point that Magic had known as a basketball player, on any level. Many fans felt that his decision to take the final shot rather than pass the ball confirmed Nixon's criticisms.

There was little doubt that Johnson's performance in Game 3 was his worst as a professional. He shot a sickening 2 for 14 from the floor and missed 2 of 3 crucial free throws just 30 seconds before his failure at the buzzer. Some wags took to calling him Tragic Johnson.

Magic returned for the 1981–82 season determined to redeem himself and his team. He had never especially liked to run as a conditioning exercise, but jogging had been a crucial part of his rehabilitation from his knee injury, and he now made it central

Larry Bird (far right) tries to separate his rival and good friend from Danny Ainge (second from left) moments after the Boston Celtics guard fouled Johnson hard in Game 1 of the 1985 NBA finals. The hotly contested series—"There was no love lost between the two ballclubs," Magic recalled—provided the Lakers with a chance to avenge their loss to the Celtics in the decisive game of the 1984 championships.

to his training regimen. He arrived in training camp in the best shape of his life. Yet the fast start he had envisioned for himself and the Lakers did not materialize.

During the off-season, Dr. Jerry Buss, the team's owner, had extended Johnson's contract beyond its scheduled expiration date in 1984. The new agreement was extraordinary by the standards of the day: Magic was to receive $25 million, to be paid out over the course of 25 years. The contract was a personal-services agreement with Buss, not with the Lakers; at the end of his playing days, Johnson would work for the owner in some unspecified capacity. Many people speculated that Magic had been promised a job with the Lakers front office—as general manager, perhaps, or even as team president.

The new deal created renewed mistrust between Johnson and his teammates. Abdul-Jabbar regarded it as a violation of a personal understanding between himself and the Los Angeles management that he would always be the highest-paid Laker. Other team members had always felt uneasy about the close personal relationship between Buss and Johnson; the owner and the star guard often socialized together, and Magic was a frequent guest in Buss's home.

Johnson's teammates wondered whether the new contract blurred the line between ownership and talent. Was Magic one of them, or was he a front-office employee? Would he be advising Buss on trades and other decisions that could affect their careers? Could he be trusted?

The players' problems in regaining the closeness of their championship season were made worse by the difficulties they were experiencing on the floor. In the opinion of many of them, Magic included, the greatest problem was Westhead. Johnson believed that the coach was now a man "consumed by the need for total control"; the "unique self-effacing and homespun approach" that had made him so popular with his players during his first year at the Lakers helm was a thing of the past.

Westhead now rarely talked to his players, except during games, and he disdained their advice at all times. Even worse, he had installed a highly structured half-court offense that put the reins on the Lakers' vaunted fastbreak. No longer did Johnson and Nixon have the option to create and improvise as part of the team's running game. Westhead wanted them to run his carefully orchestrated offense, the mandatory first requirement of which was to try to get the ball to Abdul-Jabbar, on every possession.

The new offense left all the Lakers, with the possible exception of the big center, extremely frustrated. The players felt hamstrung. The team's greatest assets—speed and quickness, the ability to react and make instantaneous decisions—were being taken away from it, not by a tough defense but by their own coach.

To make matters worse, Abdul-Jabbar's effectiveness was lessened, not heightened. When the Lakers had been allowed to utilize all their weapons, they had diminished the attention opponents could pay to the peerless skyhooker. But now the other teams

Johnson gives Kareem Abdul-Jabbar a giant hug after the Lakers clinch the 1985 NBA championship over the Boston Celtics. The triumph was especially sweet because it marked the first time in eight tries that Los Angeles defeated Boston in the finals and the first time ever that the Celtics lost the last game of a championship series at home.

knew that Abdul-Jabbar was always the first option in the Lakers offense, and they planned their defensive strategy accordingly.

Featuring an offense that was stagnant and predictable, Los Angeles lost four of its first six games. The defeats left a shackled Johnson feeling "humiliated." He pointed out that "players have a feel for the game, a feel for what's happening on the court that coaches can't possibly have." But Westhead continued to reject his players' suggestions. His response to their assertions that the offense was not working was invariably the same: It will if you run it right.

Though the Lakers righted themselves to win five straight after the slow start, the players knew that the team was still performing poorly, and frustration continued to mount. Immediately following the team's 11th game, Westhead berated Johnson for allegedly not paying attention in a huddle and for what he regarded as an ongoing poor attitude. The attack left Magic furious. "Basketball is my life," he has often said, and no one had ever criticized his commitment to winning. To his teammates and journalists in the locker room afterward, Johnson said that since the situation was irreparable, he wanted to be traded.

Buss responded by firing Westhead. The owner, who insisted that the decision had been reached several days before Johnson's outburst, did not enjoy the style of ball his team was playing any more than his players did, and he desired a return to Showtime. Nevertheless, most observers regarded the timing of the announcement as more than a coincidence. If Johnson himself had not actually fired the coach, it was said, he had gotten Westhead fired.

The questions regarding the star's relationship to management were raised anew. Even Jamaal Wilkes, one of the players who had been unhappy with Westhead, wondered, "If [Magic] got mad at a player, would he be gone the next day?"

Johnson's already somewhat tarnished public image lost a little more of its luster. He was portrayed in the press as overpaid and spoiled, the enthusiastic, smiling college star having been inevitably corrupted by the big money and cynicism of the pro game. At the first Los Angeles home game after Westhead's ouster, Magic was vociferously booed, and catcalls and taunts followed him around the league.

The criticism hurt, but the firing of Westhead proved to be the best thing possible for Johnson's professional career. Buss named Pat Riley, who had been Westhead's assistant, as the Lakers' new head coach. The intense Riley was a devotee of the running game, an advocate of what he called "freedom with control" for his players on the court, and he believed that all the control his supremely talented squad needed existed in the person of Magic Johnson. Riley was the first of Johnson's coaches to fully appreciate the genius of his game, to recognize that the spectacular behind-the-back dribbles and spinning whirls into the lane were informed by an understanding of the game as profound as any coach's. He called Magic a "fundamentally flamboyant" player, and in a short time Showtime was in high gear once again at the Forum.

Unleashed, the Lakers reclaimed the NBA championship in 1982 and went to the finals again in 1983, where there was no shame in being defeated by an even better Philadelphia team than the one Los Angeles had beaten the year before. Showtime made the Lakers the most popular and glamorous team in the league. And Riley, whose own considerable substance as a coach was often overshadowed by his fashionable style—his black hair was always hiply slicked back, and he wore only elegantly designed Giorgio Armani suits on the sideline—gave much of the credit for the team's success to Magic, who received the Most Valuable Player Award for the 1982 playoffs.

"Magic," Riley observed, "has taken it upon himself to give the team what it needs. His impact on a game is incredible. Because of his great intelligence, court sense, and instinct, he never comes downcourt with a preconceived sense of what to do. Like, he doesn't come down figuring, 'Okay, I'm going to shoot this one,' and block out all other options. He looks around, sizes up the situation, and makes the play. Almost always he makes the right one. If he were selfish, he would score 30 every night. But he knows that is unnecessary. He only takes what is there. Only when the game hangs in balance does he intently look for the shot, and that's when I want him to look for it. He's the most disciplined offensive player I've ever seen."

Johnson instructs a gym filled with youngsters at his 1986 basketball camp in Los Angeles. "Most of the kids who come to the camps are surprised about the amount of hard work I ask them to do," Magic said. "That's because it's hard for most people to know the hard work needed to play the game really well."

No one enjoyed Showtime more than Johnson. "To me," he said, "it's the greatest high in basketball. There you are in the middle on the break, getting set to create something. It's almost like dancing to music, and this is a boogie-woogie team. We might all have our own styles, but as a team we dance real well."

Despite a couple of changes in the starting lineup—second-year man James Worthy replaced the aging Jamaal Wilkes, and rookie Byron Scott took over in the backcourt for the traded Norm Nixon—the Lakers continued apace through the 1983–84 season. Worthy showed immediate signs of stardom, and Scott displayed promise. Magic dislocated a finger in January and missed nearly a month of play, but he returned in time to pass for an all-time NBA record of 22 assists in the All-Star Game and to assist on the skyhook with which Abdul-Jabbar surpassed Wilt Chamberlain for the most points scored in league history. By the schedule's end, the Lakers had won 54 games and had captured their third straight division title.

The team's fans and players were growing accustomed to such success. The Los Angeles victories in the preliminary rounds of the 1984 playoffs were hailed less for their crisp efficiency than for the eagerly anticipated championship showdown they made possible: the Lakers versus the Celtics. Bird and Johnson, as professionals, had yet to meet in the playoffs, which hoops fans rightly regard as the true crucible of NBA talent. For all the broadcasting gabble and the many inches of newsprint devoted to the series before it began, Magic summed up the showdown's appeal best: "Me and Larry at last."

Bird's Celtics had won one less championship than Johnson's Lakers: Boston had taken the title in 1981, the year of Magic's knee injury and poor performance against the Houston Rockets. Yet Bird had enjoyed an even greater degree of personal success in the NBA than had his Los Angeles rival. The Celtics star had experienced none of the trouble with coaches, teammates, fans, and the media that Johnson had been subjected to, and though some argued that the public was quicker to acclaim the achievements of a white superstar than a black one, there was no gainsaying Bird's ability. In his professional career, which like Magic's was in its fifth year, he had averaged well over 20 points and 10 rebounds a game, and he had lifted the Celtics from a brief and uncharacteristic stay at the bottom of the NBA standings to the league's upper echelon.

The 1983–84 regular season had been Bird's best yet, and he had been rewarded for his magnificent play with the league's Most Valuable Player Award, an honor Johnson had yet to reap. Bird, in fact, would go on to win the MVP Award each of the next two years. In so doing, he would become the first non-center in NBA history to win the award three times.

The debate over which of the two, Magic or Bird—there were no other viable candidates—was the league's best all-around player was passionate and entertaining. A consensus would probably have given the nod to the Celtic. And after the hard-fought, seven-game 1984 finals, few among those who formed the largest television audience ever to watch an NBA championship series and those who turned out for the games in person would have had reason to argue with that conclusion.

In creaky Boston Garden, with Johnson scoring 18 points and handing out 10 assists, many of them to Abdul-Jabbar, who led all scorers with 32, the Lakers won a close first contest.

Game 2, also in Boston, was a nip-and-tuck struggle from the outset. With a small lead in the game's last minute, the Lakers committed several horrendous turnovers that allowed Boston to tie the score. Even so, with 10 seconds left, the Lakers had the ball and a chance to win. But Johnson, while dribbling the ball and trying to determine whether to pass to Abdul-Jabbar or take the deciding shot himself, inexplicably did neither. The clock ran out as he was bouncing the ball harmlessly some 20 feet from the basket, seemingly unaware of the time remaining.

The Lakers went on to drop the game in overtime, flubbing a priceless opportunity to take two games on Boston's home court. Most of those who watched the contest felt that the Lakers had by far enjoyed the best of the play in the series, with their fast break at times threatening to overwhelm the Celtics. The series remained close only because of Los Angeles's failure in crucial moments.

The notion that the Lakers were the better team seemed to be confirmed by the results of Game 3. Back in the Forum, the Lakers ran past the Celtics by a 137–104 score, with Johnson passing for 21 assists, an NBA finals record. If in the minds of some the rout confirmed the superiority of Showtime, Bird thought that the fault was with himself and his teammates. "We played like sissies," he said. "I know the heart and soul of this team, and today the heart wasn't there, that's for sure. I can't believe a team

About to retire from basketball, Kareem Abdul-Jabbar (left) is greeted by a familiar face—a Jabbar-masked Johnson—in front of the Lakers bench in April 1989. "A lot of people will remember Kareem for his skyhook and all the points he scored," Magic said of the NBA's all-time leading scorer. "I'll remember him as a great friend and teacher."

like this would let L.A. come out and push us around like they did."

The response of his teammates to Bird's words changed the tenor of the series. The defining moment came when Kevin McHale, trailing the Lakers' Kurt Rambis on a fast break in Game 4, clotheslined the forward and sent him flying into the stanchion that supports the basket. McHale's foul was in flagrant disregard of the letter and spirit of the NBA rule book, but it was intended to send a message to the Lakers: Showtime was over. If the Lakers wanted to go to the hoop, they were going to get fouled—hard—every time.

Moments after the McHale-Rambis incident, Bird and Abdul-Jabbar went toe-to-toe in a shouting match, their faces contorted in rage, and had to be separated by the officials. Boston's physical play continued, and it had a perceptible effect on Los

Angeles's game. Celtics forward Cedric Maxwell described the change in his opponents: "Before, the Lakers were just running across the street whenever they wanted. Now, they stop at the corner, push the button, wait for the light, and look both ways."

After trailing all contest, Boston tied the score in Game 4 on a Bird jump shot with 16 seconds remaining. Los Angeles had a chance to take the last shot, but Johnson, as he had done in Game 2, wasted too much time dribbling. He finally tried to get the ball to Worthy, but his weak pass was picked off. In overtime, with 35 seconds to go and the score again tied, Magic missed two foul shots, and the Celtics went on to win Game 4. Boston then took two of the three remaining contests, with Magic making a crucial mistake in Game 7 by allowing Dennis Johnson to steal the ball from him at a critical juncture.

This time, all the team and personal accolades belonged to Bird. The Celtics were the NBA champions, and he was honored as the MVP of the playoffs. In the championship series, he had averaged a magnificent 27 points and 14 rebounds, a performance that made him the acknowledged top player in the game. Even Jerry West, the Lakers general manager, seemed to give Bird the edge in the speculative head-to-head matchup with Magic: "Bird whets your appetite for the game. He's such a great passer, and he doesn't make mistakes. Magic handles the ball more, and he makes more mistakes because he has it more. . . . The one that best approaches the kind of game I would recommend a young player model himself after is Bird. He's a genius on the floor."

Though Johnson had passed for an NBA record 95 assists in the course of the seven games, his uncharacteristic failures at crucial moments revived the old Tragic Johnson criticisms. He later described the summer that followed the series as "the worst of my life. It was the low point of my career."

Magic's nadir coincided with the NBA's ascension, a rise in popularity that has still not reached its zenith. Sparked by fan interest in the rivalry between the Lakers and the Celtics and in the selfless, enthusiastic play of Bird and Johnson, the league had begun to enjoy a spectacular popular revival. Ratings for telecasts were up, arenas were packed around the circuit, and by the end of the decade NBA games were even being broadcast regularly to more than 90 countries overseas, including Armenia, Greenland, Kuwait, and Zimbabwe. This phenomenal growth was directly attributable to the cachet Magic and Bird had given professional basketball. As a result, the late 1980s and early 1990s constituted a golden age for the NBA.

And the most glittering of the stars was Magic Johnson. He and his teammates began the second half of the 1980s by dedicating the 1984–85 season to revenging themselves on Boston. In 1985, Los Angeles won its division once more—as it had done every season since Magic's disastrous second campaign in the NBA, and as it would do each year through 1990—and stormed through the playoffs to set up another confrontation with the Celtics, who had compiled the best regular-season record in the league.

After a record-shattering Boston victory in Game 1 by a stunning 148–114 score, Los Angeles regrouped to take four of the next five games and reclaim the crown. It marked the first time in the history of the two franchises that the Lakers had beaten the Celtics in a playoff series. To make matters sweeter for Johnson and his teammates, the clinching victory took place on the parquet floor of the Boston Garden.

This time, Magic had played a nearly flawless series. But in his own mind true redemption for his poor performance in the 1984 finals did not come until 1987, when the Lakers defeated the Celtics in what was destined to be their last playoff matchup during the Bird-Johnson era. (After a successful 1986 regular season, Magic and the Lakers had been ousted from the playoffs by a tall and talented Houston squad; Boston had gone on to regain the title.)

The 1987 season was Johnson's greatest as a professional to date. For the first time, in the face of Abdul-Jabbar's eroding talents, Magic was called upon to become Los Angeles's leading scorer—a challenge he met readily. In fact, Johnson's superb all-around play won him awards as the most valuable player of both the regular season and the playoffs—a tandem accolade that only four men before him, including Bird, had won.

Johnson's clutch play in the championship series, including his famed "junior, junior skyhook" over Parish and McHale—a shot that Magic describes as the most memorable of his career—won him innumerable compliments. But it was Bird's description of him as "a perfect player" that he most cherished. It was a characterization that he had worked hard to deserve—"Calling him Magic somehow suggests he's doing it with tricks instead of hard work and fundamentals and knowledge of the game," Pat Riley pointed out—and having it come from the player he admired most made it all the more meaningful. ❧

8

OVERTIME

A<small>S</small> THE 1991–92 NBA regular season approached, Magic Johnson enjoyed a unique status among the league's superstars. He was a perennial all-star—indeed, he had been invited to play in the All-Star Game every year he had been in the league, and he had been named to the All-NBA First Team every season from 1983 onward. He had also passed for more assists than anyone in the history of the game.

Yet Johnson's reputation owed more to his contributions to collective accomplishments than to any specific individual achievements, as numerous and grand as his were. Simply put, he had logged more winning time than anyone else in the league. In large part because of his approach, the players as well as the fans had come to regard the number of championships a person won (as opposed to any statistical feat) as the supreme measure of his career. Magic was able to flash more championship rings than anyone: five.

Johnson had won his fifth NBA title with the Lakers in 1988, when they had triumphed over the bruising Detroit Pistons, a team built around excellent defense, extremely physical play, and the multifarious talents of Isiah Thomas, a diminutive guard whose wondrous play caused him to be nicknamed

Johnson puts a move on fellow NBA superstar Michael Jordan. "I have the nickname Magic," Johnson said, "but every player in the NBA is a Magician. To play the game and play it well, we all need a few tricks, a bit of basketball sleight of hand."

Pocket Magic. (The extremely close friendship between Johnson and Thomas had given rise to a unique custom: before the tip-off of each game between Detroit and Los Angeles, the two men kissed, "a pregame salute," said Magic, "to our friendship and our respect for the game.")

The Pistons had risen to succeed the Celtics as the Lakers' fiercest rivals, and in the two seasons that followed, they would succeed Los Angeles as NBA champions. But in 1988 they were not yet quite ready to ascend to the throne. The Lakers' triumph enabled Johnson and his teammates to accomplish something that no one in the NBA had been able to do since Bill Russell and the Celtics in 1969: win back-to-back championships.

In 1989, the Pistons foiled the Lakers' attempt to "three-peat," in part because a hamstring injury prevented Johnson from playing more than a few minutes in the championship series. Nevertheless, Magic was still honored with the league's 1989 MVP Award, an accolade he claimed again in 1990, when the Lakers were eliminated early in the playoffs. In 1991, a year when analysts were predicting the demise of the Lakers dynasty, Magic amassed the highest single-season assists total of his career and led the team back to the championship round, where they were defeated by a Chicago Bulls squad spearheaded by Michael Jordan.

It is a mark of Johnson's influence on the game that it took Jordan's winning a championship before many people would fully acknowledge the Chicago star's greatness, even though he had already won five scoring championships and his inimitable tongue-wagging dunks and serpentine drives dominated the league's highlight reels. Magic's five championship rings and nine trips to the finals had become the standard against which a new generation of NBA players measured greatness, just as Bill Russell's 11

Johnson introduces his 10-year-old son, Andre Mitchell, to the crowd at the Los Angeles Forum on February 16, 1992, during the halftime ceremony to retire Magic's jersey number, 32. The Lakers star had ended his career with the team three months earlier, after announcing to the public that he had been infected with the human immunodeficiency virus (HIV), which causes acquired immune deficiency syndrome (AIDS).

championships in his 13 seasons with the Celtics had been the yardstick for an earlier generation.

Johnson enjoyed a unique stature off the court as well. In Los Angeles, that most star-struck of American cities, he was the luminary that the Oscar winners and Grammy nominees craned their heads to see when he entered a restaurant. His endorsement deals with Pepsi, Kentucky Fried Chicken, and Spalding earned him close to $12 million a year—much more than he earned in salary from the Lakers. He invested his money wisely, and profits from his sports apparel company and Pepsi-Cola distributorship brought in more millions. All told, he enjoyed a level of business success that was unprecedented for a black American athlete.

"I was given the gifts to become not only an athlete," Johnson told *Sports Illustrated* in 1990, "but also a businessman, a thinker who could help dispel the myth that most athletes are dumb jocks who can't see beyond the next game. I'm glad that I have earned about $12 million annually in endorsement income in recent years but I'm happier about the fact that my business success has helped so many young blacks to learn that they can become entrepreneurs, and if they play ball, they can be both athletes and businessmen." Aware that blacks had traditionally been grossly underrepresented in the ownership and management ranks of professional basketball, even though they dominated the game itself, Johnson aspired to ownership of the Lakers or another NBA franchise.

The money made possible an extremely comfortable life-style, centered around Johnson's house (which features an indoor basketball court for late-night shoot-arounds) high in the hills overlooking Los Angeles. He also bought a home for his parents and otherwise eased their financial worries.

Johnson's hefty earnings also made possible a commitment to charity matched by few other professional athletes. The foremost of his numerous charitable endeavors was his association with the United Negro College Fund (UNCF). For many years, Magic hosted and organized an off-season all-star game called "A Midsummer Night's Magic," as well as a number of fund-raising banquets attended by his fellow NBA stars. All the proceeds from the banquets and the game (which has become the NBA's premier off-season event, played always before a capacity crowd eager to see, for example, Magic and Bird together on the same team) are donated to the UNCF. To date, Magic has raised more than $5 million for the fund. In addition, he personally donated more than $100,000 each year to Rust College, a black educational institution in Mississippi.

In the summer preceding the 1991–92 season, the 32-year-old Johnson took on a new role: the NBA's unofficial overseas ambassador. By the 1990s, basketball had become, next to soccer, the world's most popular team sport (it is expected to overtake soccer by the year 2000), and the NBA was enjoying a corresponding surge in international popularity that coincided with Magic's time as a professional, particularly in Europe. Just as the best European professional players aspired to play in the NBA—and by the 1990s, several had fulfilled their dream, including Magic's teammate on the Lakers, the Serbian center Vlade Divac—continental hoops aficionados regarded the NBA as the highest expression of the art of roundball.

The news that for the first time a team of NBA all-stars would represent the United States in the basketball competition at the Summer Olympic Games—to be held in 1992 at Barcelona, Spain—therefore met with much excitement and anticipation. When construction of the stadium that would host the competition was finished in Barcelona, Magic was asked to sink the ceremonial first lay-up. Further indication of his international popularity was evident in the acclaim that the French showered upon him when he and the Lakers visited Paris in the late summer of 1991 for a four-team international tournament, which Los Angeles won easily. The French press referred to him simply as the Master.

Johnson would soon receive much more media attention. At three o'clock on the afternoon of Thursday, November 7, 1991, during the first week of the NBA season, he held a press conference at the Forum. He spoke briefly to the assembled throng of reporters and NBA officials, many of whom seemed more overwhelmed by Magic's statement than he did.

The magic is back: Johnson caps off the first stage of his comeback from retirement by capturing the 1992 NBA All-Star Game's Most Valuable Player Award. Celebrating the honor with him are his wife, Cookie (second from right), and his parents, Christine (far right) and Earvin, Sr. (far left).

Because he had been infected with the human immunodeficiency virus (HIV), he said, he would be retiring from the NBA. HIV causes acquired immune deficiency syndrome (AIDS), a disease that is usually sexually transmitted. To this date, AIDS is still incurable and is, over time, always fatal.

The statement made the front pages of every newspaper in the country and was at the top of every television newscast: The NBA's greatest player had announced not only the end of his career but, it seemed, the end of his life.

Johnson himself seemed to be one of the few who regarded the circumstances as something less than tragic. The presence of HIV in a person is a precursor of AIDS, his physicians pointed out, not the disease itself. Magic was still an extremely healthy, fit individual whose lifelong devotion to physical conditioning gave reason for a cautious optimism that he would continue to enjoy good health for years. His retirement was more a precautionary step—taken on the advice of his physicians, who were unsure how his body would respond to the physical stress of an NBA season—than an immediate necessity.

Somehow managing several of his famous smiles, Johnson assured his questioners that the apparent end of his basketball career in no way meant the end of his life, which he intended to keep on enjoying. Even "if I die tomorrow," he added, "I've had the greatest life anybody could imagine. I've lived a life that no one could have imagined for me or anybody else."

The purpose of that life, Johnson declared, would now be to educate Americans about AIDS. Because the primary means of AIDS transmission in the United States has been homosexual sexual activity, the illness has been stigmatized, regarded as not essentially threatening to those who engage in heterosexual behavior, and those who suffer from its ravages have been shunned as outcasts and pariahs. Amid speculation that his being HIV-positive was tantamount to a declaration of homosexuality, Magic acknowledged that he had obtained the virus as the result of promiscuous sexual activity, but of an exclusively heterosexual variety.

The import of his announcement, Johnson worked hard to make clear in the months following his retirement—through talk show appearances, his work with a special presidential council on AIDS, the production of an educational television show aimed at youngsters, and a book on how to prevent the disease intended for young readers—was that any sexual behavior in which there is a possible exchange of bodily fluids, be it among members of the same sex or members of opposite sexes, puts an individual at risk of contracting the virus. It matters little whether one is gay or not, Magic said; no one was immune from AIDS.

It was a message Johnson worked exceptionally hard to impart to young people. Learn safe, responsible sexual behavior, he urged.

Magic's own irresponsibility had harmed more people than just himself, he acknowledged; there was no way of telling how many women he had infected with the virus, and it was only through the greatest of good fortune that his wife, Earletha Kelley, called Cookie, a college sweetheart whom he had married in the summer of 1991, and their newborn son, Earvin Johnson III, born in June 1992, were not also infected. (A child can be born with the virus if the mother is infected.)

Magic's prominence as perhaps America's foremost sporting hero ensured that his message would not go unheard. According to Michael Weinstein, head of the AIDS Healthcare Foundation, "The main thing that raises awareness of the HIV virus or AIDS is to know someone who has it. Now everybody in America knows someone with HIV." Johnson hoped that his popularity as a public figure would help erase the stigma that is sometimes attached to those with AIDS. "No one has to run from me," he said. "When you see me, you can still ask for autographs and high fives. I'm going to be the same guy I've always been. I'm not all of a sudden someone you should be afraid of being around."

Though it seemed that for Johnson the games were essentially over, he left the NBA with the same grace with which he performed on its hardwood floors for 12 seasons. As always, there was enthusiasm and high spirits, and he displayed no regret or bitterness. "I can't look at this infection as anything other than an opportunity to do something that might wind up overshadowing basketball," he said. "It's not easy to accept . . . and sure, I was convinced that I would never catch the AIDS virus, but if it was going to happen to someone, I'm actually glad it happened to me. I think I'll be able to spread the message concerning AIDS better than anyone."

His friends emphasized that for Magic, who had always worked the clock so well, there was still plenty of time left. Pat Riley, one of the few—along with Larry Bird and Isiah Thomas—whom Magic had told of his condition prior to the dramatic press conference, said, "We don't want to eulogize him. His career is over in basketball but his life goes on."

There was even time to take a few final shots. In an unprecedented testimony to his stature in the game to which he had devoted his life, Johnson was voted by the fans to the starting lineup of the 1992 All-Star Game even though he had not played in a single contest all year. The master of the dramatic play then walked away with the MVP honor for the game, in which he passed for nine assists, many of them in trademark spectacular fashion, and scored 25 points, including three straight three-point baskets in the game's closing minutes. Though there were still several seconds left on the game clock, Magic's colleagues simply walked off the court following his last basket, thereby ending the game, as if in immediate silent unison that the last successful exercise of that arcing, somewhat awkward shot of his—still much closer in form to an old-style set shot than the Dave Bing jump shot he had so admired as a boy—should be their final memory of Magic Johnson on an NBA court.

But there were still more exhibitions to come. In July 1992, Johnson attained the one basketball award that had eluded him: a gold medal in the Olympic Games. As cocaptain (with Bird) and floor leader, he led the powerhouse USA basketball team to a succession of overwhelming victories at Barcelona. Hyped as the Dream Team, the U.S. squad was

Johnson cocaptains the U.S. men's basketball squad to a gold medal at the 1992 Summer Olympic Games. Except for the Dream Team, he said, "I've always been the underdog. Every team I've been on wasn't supposed to win. Even when I go to the playgrounds I don't necessarily pick the best players. I always pick the players who want to work hard."

perhaps the most powerful assemblage of basketball talent ever. Rising to the occasion, Johnson shone the brightest even among these stars.

"It's Magic's team," Michael Jordan admitted, and Johnson ran it as brilliantly as he had ever done the Lakers, the Michigan State Spartans, or the Everett Vikings, pushing the ball relentlessly upcourt, looking one way and passing another, taking it to the rack with a hoopsy-doopsy flourish, punctuating a basket with an ear-to-ear grin and a high-five for a teammate. On the court at Barcelona, things seemed very simple, as they always had for Magic on the hardwood. "This," he said, "is where I belong."

Meanwhile, back in the United States, several huge chains of bookstores were refusing to stock Johnson's book *What You Can Do To Avoid AIDS* because of its forthright discussion of sexual behavior. Certain opinion makers were also condemning the basketball great as a role model because of his admittedly promiscuous past. Johnson stirred further controversy by resigning from the AIDS commission, charging that President George Bush had "dropped the ball" by ignoring its recommendations. In addition, the wisdom of his returning to NBA competition was debated after Magic stated that he was considering a comeback.

That debate intensified after September 29, 1992, when Magic announced that he was rejoining the Lakers as a player for the upcoming season. "Everybody who knows me knows that on the court is where I belong," he said on that day, but not everyone agreed with him. Despite the assertions of physicians that the risk of another player's contracting HIV from Johnson was infinitesimal, several NBA players had misgivings about taking the court with him, and they made their feelings known. So, after a successful training camp and preseason in which he demonstrated anew every facet of his on-court brilliance, on November 2, Magic once again announced his retirement from the NBA, citing the "controversies" that surrounded his return.

While AIDS activists denounced the reaction of Johnson's colleagues as yet another tragic example of the kind of prejudice HIV-positive individuals face all too often in the workplace, for Magic the integrity of the game to which he had dedicated his life was paramount. "His feeling was that it could affect the outcome of a ballgame if players were afraid to play against him, and he didn't want that," his agent, Lou Rosen, said. "Maybe he retired because he loves the game too much." ❧

APPENDIX:
CAREER STATISTICS

————————— ◖◗ —————————

REGULAR SEASON

(LOS ANGELES LAKERS)

YEAR	G	MIN AVG	FG	FGA	FG PCT	FTA	FTM	FT PCT	REB	REB AVG	AST	AST AVG	STL	PTS	AVG
1979-80	77	36.3	503	949	53.0	374	462	81.0	596	7.7	563	7.3	187	1,387	18.0
1980-81	37	37.1	312	587	53.2	171	225	76.0	320	8.6	317	8.6	127	798	21.6
1981-82	78	38.3	556	1,036	53.7	329	433	76.0	751	9.6	743	9.5	208	1,447	18.6
1982-83	79	36.8	511	933	54.8	304	380	80.0	683	8.6	829	10.5	176	1,326	16.8
1983-84	67	38.3	441	780	56.5	290	358	81.0	491	7.3	875	13.1	150	1,178	17.6
1984-85	77	36.1	504	899	56.1	391	464	84.3	476	6.2	968	12.6	113	1,406	18.3
1985-86	72	35.8	483	918	52.6	378	434	87.1	426	5.9	907	12.6	113	1,354	18.8
1986-87	80	36.3	683	1,308	52.2	535	631	84.8	504	6.3	977	12.2	138	1,909	23.9
1987-88	72	36.6	490	996	49.2	417	489	85.3	449	6.2	858	11.9	114	1,408	19.6
1988-89	77	37.5	579	1,137	50.9	513	563	91.1	607	7.9	988	12.8	138	1,730	22.5
1989-90	79	37.2	546	1,138	48.0	567	637	89.0	522	6.6	907	11.5	132	1,765	22.3
1990-91	79	37.1	466	976	47.7	519	573	90.6	551	7.0	989	12.5	102	1,531	19.4
1995-96	32	29.9	137	294	46.6	201	172	85.6	183	5.7	220	6.9	26	468	14.6
TOTALS	906	36.4	6,211	11,951	52.0	4,989	5,821	85.7	6,596	7.3	10,141	11.1	1,724	17,707	19.5

PLAYOFFS

(LOS ANGELES LAKERS)

YEAR	G	MIN AVG	FG	FGA	FG PCT	FTA	FTM	FT PCT	REB	REB AVG	AST	AST AVG	STL	PTS	AVG
1979-80	16	41.1	103	199	51.8	85	106	80.2	168	10.5	151	9.4	49	293	18.3
1980-81	3	42.3	19	49	38.8	13	20	65.0	41	13.7	21	7.0	8	51	17.0
1981-82	14	40.1	83	157	52.9	77	93	82.8	158	11.3	130	9.3	40	243	17.4
1982-83	15	42.9	100	206	48.5	68	81	84.0	128	8.5	192	12.8	34	268	17.9
1983-84	21	39.9	151	274	55.1	80	100	80.0	139	6.6	284	13.5	42	382	18.2
1984-85	19	36.2	116	226	51.3	100	118	84.7	134	7.1	289	15.2	32	333	17.5
1985-86	14	38.6	110	205	53.7	82	107	76.6	100	7.1	211	15.1	27	302	21.6
1986-87	18	37.0	146	271	53.9	98	118	83.1	139	7.7	219	12.2	31	392	21.8
1987-88	24	40.2	169	329	51.4	132	155	85.2	130	5.4	303	12.6	34	477	19.9
1988-89	14	37.0	85	174	48.9	78	86	90.7	83	5.9	165	11.8	27	258	16.4
1989-90	9	41.8	76	155	49.0	70	79	88.6	57	6.3	115	12.8	11	227	25.2
1990-91	19	43.3	118	268	44.0	157	178	88.2	154	8.1	240	12.6	23	414	21.8
TOTALS	186	39.8	1,276	2,513	50.8	1,040	1,241	83.8	1,431	7.7	2,320	12.5	358	3,640	19.6

CHRONOLOGY

1959   Born Earvin Johnson, Jr., in Lansing, Michigan, on August 14

1975   Nicknamed Magic by a local sportswriter; named first-team all-state selection as a high school sophomore

1977   Leads Everett High School Vikings to the state championship; enrolls at Michigan State University

1978   Selected to the All–Big Ten Team; declines to enter the NBA draft

1979   Leads the Michigan State Spartans to the NCAA championship; named to *The Sporting News* All-American first team; named NCAA Division I Tournament Most Outstanding Player; enters the NBA draft and is made the number one pick by the Los Angeles Lakers

1980   Lakers win the NBA championship; Johnson wins the playoff's Most Valuable Player Award; named to the All-Rookie Team

1981   Leads the NBA in steals; son, Andre Mitchell, is born

1982   Johnson leads the NBA in steals; named to the All-NBA second team; Lakers win the NBA championship; Johnson wins the playoff's Most Valuable Player Award

1983   Hands out an all-time NBA record of 22 assists at the All-Star Game; leads the NBA in assists; named to the All-NBA first team

1984   Leads NBA in assists; named to the All-NBA first team

1985   Named to the All-NBA first team; Lakers win the NBA championship

1986   Leads the NBA in assists; named to the All-NBA first team

1987   Leads the NBA in assists; named to the All-NBA first team; wins the playoff's Most Valuable Player Award; Lakers win the NBA championship; Johnson wins the NBA's Most Valuable Player Award

1988   Named to the All-NBA first team; Lakers win the NBA championship

1993   Comes out of retirement and begins season with the Lakers, but a month later again retires

1994   Coaches the Lakers for the last 16 games of the season; purchases share of the team and becomes part owner

1995   Opens a chain of movie theaters in minority neighborhoods

1996   Plays 32 games of regular season for the Lakers, but retires after the team is ousted by Houston in the first round of the playoffs; records 138th triple-double of his career, the most in NBA history

1997   Selected to the NBA's 50th anniversary All-Time Team; signs deal with Twentieth TV, a Fox-owned syndicator, to develop, produce, and host his own late-night talk show, *The Magic Hour*

FURTHER READING

Abdul-Jabbar, Kareem, with Mignon McCarthy. *Kareem*. New York: Warner, 1990.

Axthelm, Pete. *The City Game: Basketball from the Garden to the Playground*. New York: Penguin, 1982.

Corn, Frederick Lynn. *Basketball's Magnificent Bird: The Larry Bird Story*. New York: Random House, 1982.

Gutman, Bill. *Chairmen of the Boards: Erving, Bird, Malone and Johnson*. New York: Grosset & Dunlap, 1980.

—————. *Magic: More Than a Legend*. HarperCollins, 1992.

Hollander, Zander, and Alex Sachare. *The Official NBA Basketball Encyclopedia*. New York: New American Library, 1989.

Johnson, Earvin. *What You Can Do To Avoid AIDS*. New York: Times Books, 1992.

Johnson, Earvin, and Richard Levin. *Magic*. New York: Viking, 1983.

Johnson, Earvin, and Roy S. Johnson. *Magic's Touch*. New York: Addison-Wesley, 1989.

Levine, Lee Daniel. *Bird: The Making of an American Sports Legend*. New York: McGraw-Hill, 1988.

Pascarelli, Peter. *The Courage of Magic Johnson: From Boyhood Dreams to Superstar to His Toughest Challenge*. New York: Bantam, 1992.

Stauth, Cameron. *The Golden Boys: The Unauthorized Inside Look at the U.S. Olympic Basketball Team*. New York: Simon and Schuster, 1992.

INDEX

PICTURE CREDITS
———— ❦ ————

SEAN DOLAN has a degree in literature and American history from SUNY Oswego. He is the author of many biographies and histories for young adult readers, including *James Beckwourth* in the BLACK AMERICANS OF ACHIEVEMENT SERIES, and has edited a series of volumes on the famous explorers of history.

NATHAN IRVIN HUGGINS, one of America's leading scholars in the field of black studies, helped select the titles for the BLACK AMERICANS OF ACHIEVEMENT series, for which he also served as senior consulting editor. He was the W.E.B. Du Bois Professor of History and of Afro-American Studies at Harvard University and the director of the W.E.B. Du Bois Institute for Afro-American Research at Harvard. He received his doctorate from Harvard in 1962 and returned there as a professor in 1980 after teaching at Columbia University, the University of Massachusetts, Lake Forest College, and the California State University, Long Beach. He was the author of four books and dozens of articles, including *Black Odyssey: The Afro-American Ordeal in Slavery*, *The Harlem Renaissance*, and *Slave and Citizen: The Life of Frederick Douglass*, and was associated with the Children's Television Workshop, National Public Radio, the Boston Athenaeum, the Museum of Afro-American History, the Howard Thurman Educational Trust, and Upward Bound. Professor Huggins died in 1989, at the age of 62, in Cambridge, Massachusetts.